Robert Laneham

A Letter, Whearin Part of the Entertainment untoo the Queenz Majesty

At Killingwoorth Castl in Warwick Sheer, in this Soomerz Progrest 1575

Robert Laneham

A Letter, Whearin Part of the Entertainment untoo the Queenz Majesty
At Killingwoorth Castl in Warwick Sheer, in this Soomerz Progrest 1575

ISBN/EAN: 9783744764193

Printed in Europe, USA, Canada, Australia, Japan

Cover: Foto ©ninafisch / pixelio.de

More available books at **www.hansebooks.com**

A LETTER:

WHEARIN,

Part of the ENTERTAINMENT untoo the

QUEENZ MAJESTY,

AT

Killingwoorth Castl in *Warwick Sheer,*

IN THIS

Soomerz Progreſt 1575,

IZ SIGNIFIED:

From a freend Officer attendant in the Coourt, unto his freend a *Citizen* and *Merchaunt* of *LONDON.*

De Reginâ noſtrâ illuſtriſſimâ.

Dum laniata ruant vicina ah regna tumultu,
Læta, fuos inter, genialibus ILLA diebus
(Gratia Diis,) fruitur: Rumpantur & ilia Codro.

WARWICK:

Printed by and for J. SHARP, and Sold by
Meſsrs. Rivington's *St. Pauls Church Yard,* London.
1784.
[Price EIGHTEEN-PENCE.]

Untoo my good freend, Mafter
Humfrey Martin, MERCER.

AFTER my hartie commendations,
I commend me hartily too yoo.
Underftande yee, that fins throogh
God and good freends, I am placed at
Coourt heer (as ye wot) in a woorfhipfull
room: Whearby I am not onlie acquaint-
ed with the moft, and well knoen to the beft,
and every Officer glad of my Company: But
alfo have poour, adayz (while the Councell
fits not) to go and too fee things fight wor-
thy; and too bee prezent at any Sheaw or
Spectacl, only whear this Progrefs repre-
zented unto her Highnefs: And of part of
which Sportez, having takin fum notez and
obfervationz (for I cannot bee Idl at ony
hand in the World) az well to put fro me
fufpition of Sluggardy, az too pluk from yoo
doout of ony my forgetfulnefs of Freendfhip:
I have thought it meet to impart them unto
yoo, as frankly, az freendly, and az fully as

I can;

I can: Well wot yee the blak Prins waz
never ſtained with diſloyaltee of ingratitude
towarde ony, I dare be his warrant hee will
not beginee with yoo that hath at his hand
ſo deeply dezerved. But heerin the better
for conceyving of my minde and inſtruction
of yoors, ye muſt gyve mee leave a littl, az
well to preface untoo my matter, as to
diſcoors ſumwhat of *Killyngwoorth Caſtl.*
A territory of the right honorabl, my
ſingular good Lord, my Lord the Earl of
Leyceter: of whooz incomparabl cherrying
and enterteynment thear, untoo her *Majeſty*
noow, I will ſhew yoo a part heer that coold
not ſee all; nor had I ſeen all, coold well
report the hallf. Whear Thynges for the
Parſons, for the Place, time, Coſt, deviſez,
ſtraungnes, and Aboundauns of all that ever
I ſawe (and yet have I been, what under my
Maſter Bomſted, and what on my oun affayres,
whyle I occupied Merchaundize, both in
Fraunce and *Flaunders* long and many a
day,) I ſaw none ony where ſo memorabl,
I tell you plain.

Killingwoorth The *Caſtl* hath name of *Killingwoorth,*
Caſtl. but of truth grounded upon ſeythful Storie
Kenelwoorth: It ſtonds in *Warwykſhyre,* a
lxiiii

lxxiiii myle north-weſt from *London,* and az it were in the Navel of *England,* foure myle ſumwhat South from *Coventree* a proper Cittee, and a lyke diſtaunce from *Warwyk,* a fayre Sheere toun on the North: In Ayr ſweet and hollſum, raiſed on an eazy mounted hill, iz ſette eevenlie coaſted with the froont ſtraight intoo the Eaſt, hath the Tenaunts and Tooun about it, that pleaſantly ſhifts from dale too Hyll ſundry whear wyth ſweet Springs burſting foorth: And iz ſo plentifullie well ſorted on every ſide intoo Arabl, Meads, Paſture, Wood, Water, and good Ayrz, az it appeerz to have need of nothing that may perteyn too living or pleazure. Too avauntage hath it, hard on the Weſt, ſtill nouriſht with many lively Springs, a goodly Pool of rare beauty, bredth, length, deapth, & ſtore of all kinde freſh water fiſh, delicat, great and fat, and alſo of wild fooul byſide. By a rare ſituacion & natural amitee ſcemz this Pool conjoynd to the *Caſtlz* that on the Weſt layz the head az it wear upon the *Caſtlz* booſom, embraceth it on either ſide Soouth and North with both the Arms, ſettlz it ſelf az in a reach a ſlight ſhoot brode, ſtretching foorth body and legs a myle or too Weſt-ward: Between

tween a fayre Park on the one fide, which
by the Brayz is linked too the *Caftl* on the
South, fprinckled at the entraunce with a
feaw Coonyez, that for colour and fmall-
nes of number, feem to be fuffered more for
pleafure than commoditee: And on the
oother fide, North & Weft, agoodlie chafe:
Waft, wyde, large, and full of red Deer and
oother ftately Gamez for hunting: Beautified
with many delectabl frefh and umbragioous
boowz, Arberz, Seatz, and Walks, that with
great Art, Coft, & diligens wear very plea-
fauntlie appointed: Which alfo the natural
grace by the tall and frefh fragrant treez
and foil, did fo far foorth commend, az *Diana*
her - felf myght have deyned thear well
enough too raunge for her Paftime.

The leaft Arm of this Pool North-ward
had my Lorde adoourned with a beautifull
bracelet of a fayre tymbred bridge, that iz
of xiiii foot wide, and a fix hundred foot
long; railed all on both fidez, ftrongly
planked for paffage, reaching from the Chafe
too the *Caftl:* That thus in the midft hath
clear profpect over theez pleazures on the
back part; and forward over all the Toun,
and mooch of the Countree befide.

Heertoo

Heertoo, a speciall commoditee at hand of fundrie quarriez of large building ftone, the goodnefs whearof may the eazlyar be judged, in the building and auntienty of the *Caftl;* that (az by the name and hyftories, well may be gathered) waz firft reared by *Kenulph,* and his young Sun *Kenelm:* born both indeed within the Ream heer, but yet of the race of *Saxons:* And reigned Kings of *Marchlond* from the year of our Lord 798, too 23 yeerz toogyther, above 770 yeer ago. Altho' the *Caftl* hath one Auncient ftrong and large Keep that iz called *Ceazarz Tour,* rather (az I have good cauz to think) for that it iz fquare and high, foormed after the maner of *Cezarz Fortz* then that ever he bylt it. Nay noow I am a littl in *Mafter Martin* ile tell you all.

Florilege fol. 221, & 225.

Guil. Malmefb. lib. I.

This *Marchlond* that ftoryes call *Mercia,* iz numbred in their Bookes the foourth of the feaven Kingdomes that the *Saxons* had whilom heer divided among them in the Ream: Began in *Anno Dom.* 616, one hundred and thirtie nine yeer after *Horfins* and *Hengift;* continued in the race of 17 Kings, 249 yeers togyther, and ended in *Ann.* 875. Reyzed from the reft, (fayz the

book)

book) at firſt by *Penda'z* preſumption: overthroun at laſt by *Buthred's Haſcardy,* and
Mercia. ſo fell to the kingdoom of the *Weſt-Saxons.* And *Marchlond* had in it *London, Mildelſex,* heering a Biſhoprik. Had more of *Shyrez: Gloceter, Woorceter,* and *Warwik,* and heering a Biſhoprik. *Cheſter* (that now we call *Cheſhyre)* *Darby* and *Staffoord,* whereuntoo one Biſhop that had alſo part of *Warwyk* and *Shrewſbery,* and his See at *Coventree* that was then aforetime at *Lychfeeld.* Heretoo: *Hereford,* wherein a Biſhoprik that had more too Juriſdiction, half *Shreuſbury,* part of *Warwyk* and alſo of *Gloceter,* and the See at *Hereford.* Alſo had *Oxford, Buckingham, Hertford, Huntingdon,* & halfe of *Bedforde;* and too theez, *Norhampton,* part of *Leyceter,* and alſo *Lincoln,* whearunto a Biſhop: Whoz See at *Lincoln* Citee that ſumtime before was at *Dorcheſter,* heerto the reſt of *Leyceter* and in *Nottingham,* that of old had a ſpeciall Biſhop, whooz See waz at *Leyceter;* but after, put to the charge of the Archbiſhop of *Yorke.*

Now touching the Name, that of olld Recordes I underſtand, and of Auncient Writers I find, iz call'd *Kenelworth;* Syns
moſt

moſt of the *Worth's* in *England* ſtand ny untoo like lakes, and ar eyther ſmall *Ilandz,*
ſuch one as the Seat of this *Caſtl* hath been
and eazly may bee, or is lond ground by Pool
or River whearon Willoz, Alderz, or ſuch
like doo gro: Which *Althamerus* writes Upon *Tacitus.* fol. 142.
precizely that the *Germains* cal 𝕎𝕖𝕣𝕕: Joyn- The *Germans*
ing theſe too togither with the nighneſs allſo call *Werk* that we call *Voork.*
of the Woords and ſybred of the toongs. I They call *Werlt* that we
am the bolder to pronoouns, that as our call *Woorld.*
Engliſh Woorth, with the reſt of our Auncient They *Wermut* we *Woormwood.*
Langage, was leaft us from the *Germains;* They *biel Wert* we much *Worth.*
eeven ſo that their *Werd* and our *Woorth* iz
all one thing in ſignfiaunce, common too us
both, e'en at this day: I take the caſe ſo
clern, that I ſay not az mooch az I moought.
Thus Prefice ye with the Preface; and nowe
to the Matter.

ON *Saterday* the Nyenth of *July,* at long
Ichington, a Toun & Lordſhip of my Lord's,
within a ſeaven Myle of *Killingworth,* his
Honor made her *Majeſty* great cheer at Dinner, and pleaſaunt Paſtime in Hunting by the
way after, that it was eight o'Clock in the
Evening ear her Highneſs came too *Killingwoorth:* Whear in the Park, about a flight
ſhoot from the Brayz and firſt gate of the
B *Caſtl,*

Sibyls. *Caſtl,* one the ten *Sibills,* that (we reed) wear all *Fatidicæ* and *Theobulæ,* (as parties and privy too the Gods gracious good will: (cumly clad in a Pall of white Sylk, pronounced a proper Poezi in Engliſh Rim e nd Meeter: Of effect hoow great glad eſ, her goodneſſe prezenze brought into everie Reed whear it pleazed her too cum; and ſpec a now into that place that had ſo long longed after the ſame: Ended with prophecie certain, of mooch and long profperiue he, l. and felicitee: This her *May flie* bean g y accepting, paſſed foorth untoo the next gate of the Brayz, which for the length, largenes and uſe, (as well it may ſo ſerve)

The Porter. they call now the Tylt-yard, whear a Porter, tall of Perſon, big of lim and ſtearn of coountinance, wrapt alſo all in Sylke, with a club and keiz of quantitee according, had a rough ſpeech full of Paſſions in meeter aptly made to the purpoſe: Whearby (az her Highnes was cum within his warde) hee burſt out in a great pang of impatiens to ſee ſuch uncooth trudging too and fro, ſuch riding in and out, with ſuch dyn and noiz of talk within the charge of his Offis: Whearof hee never ſaw the like nor had any warning afore, ne yet coold make too him-

ſelf

felf any cauze of the matter : At laſt upon
better vieu and aviſement, az hee preaſt too
cum neerar, confeſſing anon that hee found
himſelf pearced at the prezens of a perſonage
ſo evidently expreſſing an heroicall Soveraintee over all the whole Eſtates, and by degreez
theer biſyde, callm'd his ſtoniz, proclaims
open gates and free paſſage to all, yeelds
up a Club, his Keyz, hiz Office and all,
and on hiz kneez humbly prayz pardon of
hiz ignorauns and impaciens: which her
Highneſs graciouſlie graunting, he cauz'd
his Trumpetoourz that ſtood uppon the wall   *The Trumpetors.*
of the gate thear, too ſoound up a tune of
welcum : Which, beſyde the nobl noyz,
was ſo mooch the more pleaſaunt too behold,
becaus theez Trumpetoours, beeing ſixe in
number, wear every one an eight foot hye,
in due proportion of Parſon beſyde, all in
long garments of Sylk ſuitabl, eache with hiz
ſylvery Trumpet of a five foot long, foormed taper wyſe, and ſtraight from the upper
part untoo the neathere eend: Whear the
diameter was a 16 ynchez over, and yet ſo
temperèd by art, that being very eazy too
the blaſt, they caſt foorth no greater noyz,
nor a more unpleazaunt ſoound for time
and tune, than any oother common Trumpet,

bee

bee it never so artificially formed. Theeze
armonious blasterz, from the foreside of the
gate at her highnefs entrance whear they
began: Walking upon the Wallz untoo the
inner; had this Muzik main'eined from them
very deleftably, while her Highnefs all along
this Tylt-yard rode unto the inner gate
next the bafe Coourt of the *Cafil:* where
The Lady of the Lady of the Lake, (famous in King
the Lake.
Arthurz Book) with too *Nymphes* waiting
uppon her, arrayed all in Sylks, attending
her Highnefs comming: From the midft of
the Pool, whear upon a moovabl *Iland,*
bright blazing with Torches, fhe floting to
Land, met her *Majefty* with a well penned
meeter and matter after this fort: [* *viz*]
Firft of the Auncientee of the *Caftl,* whoo
had been ownerz of the fame e'en 'till this
day, moft alweys in the hands of the Earls of
Leyceter; hoow fhee had kept this Lake
finz King *Arthurz* Dayz; and now underftanding of her highnefs hither cumming,
thought it both office and duetie, in humble
wize to difcover her and her Eftate; offer-
ing up the fame, her Lake and Poowr there-
in, with promife of repayre unto the Coourt.
It pleazed her highnefs too thank this Lady,
and too add withall, we had thought indeed
the

the Lake had been oourz, and doo you call it yourz now? Well, we will herein common more with yoo hereafter.

THIS Pageant waz cloz'd up with a delectable harmony of Hautboiz, Shalmz, Cornets, and fuch oother looud Muzik, that held on while her *Majeſtie* pleafauntly fo paſſed from thence toward the *Caſtl* gate; whearunto from the baze Coourt over a dry valley caſt into a good foorm, waz thear framed a fayr Bridge of a twenty foot wide, *The Bridge.* and a feaventy foot long, graveld for treading, railed on either part with feaven Poſts *Seven pair of Poſts.* on a fide, that ſtood a 12 foot a funder thickned betweene with well proportioned Pillars turn'd.

UPON the firſt payr of Poſts were ſet too cumly fquare wyre Cages, a three foot long, too foot wide; and hye in them live Bitters, Curluz, Shoovelarz, Hearſheawz, Godwitz, and fuch like deinty Byrds of the prezents of *Sylvanus* the God of Foul. On the fecond *Sylvanus. 1. Prezents.* payr, too great fylver'd Bollz, featly apted too the purpoze, filde with Applz, Pearz, Cherriz, Filberdz, Walnuts, freſh upon their braunches, and with Oranges, Poungarnets, Lemmans,

Lemmans, and Pipinz, all for the giftz of
Pomona, Goddes of Fruitz. The third pair
of Posts, in too such sylver'd Bollz, had
(all in earz Green and Gld) Wheat, Barly,
Ootz, Beans and Peaz, az the gifts of *Ceres*.
The fourth Post on the least hand, in a like
sylvered Boll, had Grapes in Clusters whyte
and red, gracified with their vine leavez:
The match Post against it had a payre of
great whyte sylver lyvery Pots for Wyne:
and before them too Glassez of good capacitie,
fill'd full; the t'on with whyte Wine, the
two other with Claret; so fresh of coolor,
and of look so lovely, smiling to the Eyz of
many, that by my feith mee thought, by
their leering, they could have foound in
their harts (az the evening was hot.) to
have kist them sweetlie, and thought it no
Sin: And theez for the potencial prezents of
Bacchus the God of Wine. The fift payr had
each a fair large trey streawd with fresh grafs;
and in them, Coonger, Burt, Mullet, Fresh
Herring, Oisters, Samon, Crevis, and such
like from *Neptunus*, God of the Sea. On the
sixth payr of Posts wear set two ragged Stavez
of sylver, as my Lord givez them in Armz,
beautifully glittering of Armour thereupon
depending, Bowz, Arroz, Spearz, Sheeld,

Pomona. 2.

Ceres. 3.

Bacchus. 4.

Neptunus. 5.

Head

Head-pees, Gorget, Corfelets, Swoords, Tar-
gets, and fuch like, for *Mars* Gifts the God   *Mars.* 6.
of War. And the aptlyer (methought,) waz
it that thooz ragged Staves fupported theez
Martial prezénts, as well becauz the 'z ftaves
by their tines feem naturallie meete for the
bearing of Armoour, as alfo that they chief-
ly in this place might take upon them princi-
pall protection of her Highnefs Parfon, that
fo benignly pleazed her to take herbour.
On the feaventh Pofts, the laft and next too
the *Cyftl,* wear thear pight to faer Bay
braunches of a four foot hy, adourned on
all f.des with Lutes, Viollz, Shallmz, Cornets,
Flutes, Recorders, and Harpes, az the pre-
zents of *Phœbus* the God of Muzik for re-   *Phœbus.* 7.
joicing the mind, and alio of Phizik, for
health to the Body.

Over the *Cuftl* Gate was there faftened a
Tabl beautifully garnifht aboove with her
Highnefs Arms, and featlie with Ivy wreathz
boorded aboout, of a ten-foot Square: The
ground blak, whearupon in large white Capitall Roman fayr written, a Poem mencion-
ing theeze Gods and their Gifts, thus prezented untoo her Highnefs: Which, becauz
it remained unremooved, at leizure and
pleaze I took it oout, as foloeth.   A D

AD MAJESTATEM REGIAM.

Jupiter huc certos cernens te tendere greſſus
Cælicolas PRINCEPS aſtutum convocat Omnes:
Obſequium præſtare jubet TIBI quenque benignum.
Unde ſuas Sylvanus Aves, Pomonaque fructus,
Alma Ceres fruges, hilarantia vina Liæus,
Neptunus Piſces, tela et tutantia *Mavors*,
Suave Melos *Phœbus*, ſolidamque longamque ſalutem.
DiiTIBIREGINAhæc(cumſisDIGNISSIMA)præbent:
Hoc TIBI, cum Domino,dedit ſe & werda KENELMI.

All the Letters that mention her *Majeſty*, which
heer I put capitall, for reverens and honor wear
thear made in Golld.

But the Night well ſpent, for that theez
Verſez by torch light coold eaſily bee read,
by a Poet thearfore in a long ceruleoous
garment, with a ſide and wide ſleeves
Venecian wize drawen up to his elboz, his
dooblett ſleevez under that, Crimzen, nothing but Silke; a Bay garland on his head,
and a ſkro in his hand, making firſt an humble Obeizaunce at her highneſs cummyng,
and pointing untoo everie prezent as he
ſpake; the ſame were pronounced. Thus
viewing

viewing the Gifts, az fhe paft, and how the Pofts might agree with the fpeech of the Poet, at the eend of the bridge and entree of the Gate, waz her highnes received with a frefh delicate Armony of Flutz, in perfourmauns of *Phœbus* Prezents.

So paffing intoo the inner Coourt, her *Majefty* (that never rides but alone) thear fet doun from her palfrey, was conveied up to Chamber: When after did follo fo great a peal of gunz, and fuch lightning by fyrwork a long fpace toogither, as *Jupiter* woold fheaw himfelf too bee no further behind with hiz welcum then the reft of hiz Gods: and that woold hee have all the Countrie to kno: for indeed the noiz and flame were heard and feen a twenty myle of. Thus much *Myfter Martin* (that I remember me) for the firft daiz Bien venu. Be yee not wery, for I am fkant in the midft of my matter.

On *Sunday* the forenoon Occupied, az for the Sabot day, in quiet and vacation from woork, and in divine fervis and preaching at the Parifh Church: The Afternoon in excelent Muzik of fundry fwet Inftruments,

C

and

and in dauncing of Lordes and Ladiez, and
oother woorfhipfull degrees, uttered with
fuch lively agilitee and commendable grace
az whither it moought be more ftraunge too
the eye, or pleazunt too the minde, for my
part indeed I coold not difcern; but exceed-
ingly well was it, methought in both.

At night late, az though *Jupiter* the laft
night had forgot for bizinefs, or forborn for
curtefy and quiet, part of his wellcoom untoo her highnefs appointed, noow entrins at
the fyrft intoo hiz purpoze moderatly (az
mortallz doo) with a warning peec or too,
proceding on with incres; at laft the *Altito-
nant* difpleaz me hiz mayn poour; with blaz
of burning Darts, flying too and fro, leams
of ftarz corufcant, ftreamz and hail of firie
fparkes, lightninges of wildfier a water and
lond, flight & fhoot of thunderboltz, all with
fuch countinauns terror & vehemencie, that
the Heavins thundred, the Waters foourged;
the Earth fhooke; and in fuch fort furly, az
had we not bee affured of the fulmicant deitee waz all hot in Amitee, and could not
otherwize witneffe his wellcomming unto
her highnefs; it woold have made mee, for
my part, az hardy az I am, very veangeably
afeard

afeard. This a doo lafted while the Midnight waz paft, that well waz mee foon after
when I waz cought in my cabayn: and this
for the fecund day.

Munday was hot, and thearfore her high- *Munday*, 3.
nefs kept in a till a five a Clok in the eeven-
ing: what time it pleazz'd her too ride
foorth into the Chace too hunt the Hart of *The Hunting of the Hart fors.*
fors: which foound anon, and after fore
chafed, and chafed by the hot purfuit of the
hooundes, was fain of fine fors, at laft to
take foil. Thear to beholld the fwift fleeting of the Deer afore with the ftately Cariage
of his head in hiz fwimmyng, fpred (for the
quantitee) lyke the fail of a Ship: the
hounds harroing after, az they had bin a
number of fkiphs too the fpoyle of a Karvell:
the ton no leffe eager in purchaz of his pray,
then waz the other earneft in favegard of hiz
life: fo az the earning of the hoounds in
continuauns of their crie, the fwiftnefs of
the Deer, the running of footmen, the gallop-
ing of horfez, the blafting of hornz, the hal-
loing and hewing of the huntfmen, with the
excellent echoz between whilez from the
Woods and Waters in Valleiz refounding;
mooved Paftime deleĉtabl in fo hye a degree,

az

az for ony parſon to take pleazure by mooſt
ſenſez at onez, in mine opinion, thear can
be none ony wey comparable to this: and
ſpeciall in this place, that of nature is foormed ſo fytt for the purpoſe; in feith *Maſter*
Martin if ye coold with a Wiſh, I woold
ye had bin at it: Wel the Hart waz kild,
a goodly Deer, but ſo ceaſt not the game
yet.

· For about nien a Clock, at the hither
part of the Chaſe whear torch light attend-
ed, oout of the Woods, in her *Majeſtiez* return, rooughly came thear foorth *Hombre*
The Savage *Saluagio,* with an Oken plant pluſt up by
Man. the roots in his hande, himſelf forgrone all in
Moſs and Ivy; who, for parſonage, geſture,
and utteraunce beſide, coountenaunſt the
matter too very good liking; and had ſpeech
to effeſt: That continuing ſo long in theeze
wilde Waſtes, whearin oft had he fared both
far and neer, yet hapt he never to ſee ſo
gloríoous an Aſſemble aſore: and noow caſt
intoo great grief of mind, for that neyther
by himſelf coold he geſs, nor knew whear
elſe too bee taught, what they ſhould be,
or whoo bare eſtate. Reports ſum had he
hard many ſtraunge things, but brooyled
thearby

thearby fo mooch the more in defire of kno‑
ledge. Thus in great pangs bethought he,
and call'd he upon all his familiarz and
companionz, the Fawnz, the Satyres, the
Nymphs, the Dryades & the Hamadryades;
but none making aunfwear, whearby his
care the more encreafing, in utter grief and
extreem refuge, call'd he allowd at laft, after
hiz olld freend *Echo*,. that he wift would
hyde nothing from him, but tell him all,
if fhe wear heer. Heer (quoth *Echo*.) Heer,
Echo, and art thou thear? (fays he,) Ah
hoow mooch haft thou relieved my care‑
ful fpirits with thy curtezy onward. A my
good *Echo*, heer is a marveiloous prezenz
of dignitee; what are they I pray thee, who
is Soverain, tell me I befeech thee, or elze
hoow moought I kno? I kno (quoth fhe.)
Knoeft thou, fays he? marry that is ex‑
ceedingly well: Why then, I dezire thee,
hartily to fho mee what *Majeftie*, (for no
mean degree is it) have we heer: a *King*
or a *Queen?* (quoth *Echo*.) A *Queen!* fayez
hee? Pauzing and wifely viewing a while,
noow full certeynlie feemes thy tale to be
true: And proceeding by this maner of
Dialog. with an earneft beholding her high‑
nefs a while, recounts he firft hoow juftly

                                  that

Echo.

that foormer reports agree with his prefent fight, toouching the beautifull linaments of coountinauns, the cumly proportion of body, the Prinfly grace of prezenz, the graciouz giftz of nature, with the rare and fingular qualities of both body and mind in her *Majefty* conjoyn'd, and fo apparent at eye.. Then fhortly rehearfing Saterdaiz Aftes, of *Sibil's* falutation, of the Porter's propofition, of his Trumpetoours Muzik, of the Lake Ladiez Oration, of the feaven Godz feaven Prezentz; Hee reporteth the incredibl' joy that all cftatez in the land have allweyz of her hignes whear-foever it cums: eendeth with prefage and prayer of perpetuall felicitee, and with humble fubjaftion of him and hizzen and all that they may do. After this fort the matter went with littl differens I geffe, faving only in this point, that the thing which heer I report in unpolifht Proez, was thear pronounced in good meeter and matter, very wel indighted in rime.. *Echo* finely framed moft aptly by anfwerz thus to utter all.. And I fhall tell yoo *Mafter Martin*, by the mafs, of a mad Adventure: As this Savage for the more fubmiffion brake hiz tree afunder, and Kaft the top from him, it had almoft light upon her highnes hors hedd; whearat he ftartld,

and

the gentlman much difmayd. See the benignitee of the Prins; az the footmen lookt
well too the hors, and hee of generofitee
foon calmd of himfelf——"No hurt, "No
hurt, quoth her highnefs. Which Words
I promif yoo wee wear all glad to hear;
and took them too be the beft part of the
Play.

Tuifday, pleazaunt paffing of the time with
Muzik and dauncing; faving that toward
night it liked her *Majefty* too walk a foot
into the Chafe over the bridge: whear it
pleafed her to ftand, while upon the Pool
oout of a Barge fine appointed for the purpoze, too heer fundry kinds of very delectabl
Muzik; thus recreated, and after fum wallk
her highnes returned.

Tuifday, 4.

Wednfday, her *Majefty* rode intoo the
Chafe, a hunting again of the Hart of Fors.
The Deer, after his property, for refuge took
the foyl: but fo mafter'd by hote purfuit
on al parts, that he was taken quick in the
Pool: The Watermen held him up hard by
the hed, while at her highnes comaundment
he loft hiz earz for a raundfum and fo had
pardon for lyfe.

Wednfday, 5.

The Hart pardoned.

Thurfday,

Thurſday, 6.

A queaſt of Bearz.

Thurſday, the foourteenth of this *July,* and the fyxth day of her *Majeſtyez* cumming, a great ſort of Bandogs whear thear tyed in the utter Coourt, and thyrteen Bearz in the inner. Whooſoever made the pannell, thear wear inoow for a Queaſt, and one for challenge and need wear. A Wight of great wizdoom and gravitee ſeemed their forman to be, had it cum to a Jury: But it fell oout that they wear cauzd too appeer thear upon no ſuch matter, but onlie too aunſwear too auncient quarrell between them and the Bandogs, in a cauſe of controverſy that hath long depended, been obſtinatly full often debated with ſharp and byting argu-ments a both ſydes, and coold never be decided grown noow too ſo marveyloous a mallys, that with ſpitefull obrayds and un-charitabl chaffings alweiz they freat, az any whear the ton can heer, ſee, or ſmell the toother: And indeed at utter deadly feud. Many a maymd member, (God wot) blody-face & a torn Cote hath the quarrel coſt be-tween them, ſo far likely the leſſe yet noow to be appeazd, as thear wants not partakers too bak them a both ſidez.

Well ſyr, the Bearz wear brought foorth

intoo

intoo the Coourt, the Dogs set too them,
too argu the points eeven face too face; they
had learnd counsel also a both parts: what
may they be coounted parciall that are re-
tain but a to syde? I ween no. Very seers
both ton & toother and eager in argument:
If the Dog in pleadyng woold pluk the Bear
by the throte, the Bear with travers woould
claw him again by the scalp; Confefs and a
lift, but avoyd a coold not that waz bound too
the bar: And hiz Coounsell tolld him that
it coold be too him no pollecy in pleading.
Thearfore thus with fending and prooving,
with plucking and tugging, fkratting and
byting, by plain tooth and nayll a to side
and toother, such expens of blood and leather
waz thear between them, as a moonths licking I ween will not recoover: and yet re-
main as far out az ever they wear.

It was a sport very pleazaunt of theeze
beaftz; to fee the Bear with his pink nyez
leering after hiz enmiez approch, the nimblnefs and wayt of the Dog too take hiz a-
vauntage, and the fors and experiens of the
Bear agayn to avoyd the affauts: If he wear
bitten in one place, hoow he woold pynch
in an oother too get free: that if he wear

D   taken

taken onez, then what fhyft with byting with clawying, with roring toffing and tumbling he woold woork too wynde hym felf from them: And when he was lofe, to fhake hiz earz twyfe or thryfe wyth the blud and the flaver aboout his fiznamy, waz a matter of a goodly releef.

As this fport waz had a day time, in the *Caftl*, fo waz thear abrode at night very *un fhot and fyrework.* ftraunge and fundry kindez of fier works, compeld by cunning to fly too and fro, and too mount very hye intoo they Ayr upward, and alfo too burn unquenfhabl in the Water beneathe; contrary, ye wot, too fyerz kinde: This intermingld with a great peal of Guns, which all gave both to the ear and to the Eye the greater grace and delight, for that with fuch Order and Art they wear temper- ed, toouching time and continuaunce, that waz about too hours fpace.

Noow within alfo, in the mean time waz thear fheawed before her hignes, by an *Tumbling of the Italian.* *Italian*, fuch feats of Agilitiee, in goinges, turninges, tumblinges, caftinges, hops, jumps, leaps, fkips, fprings, gambaud, foomerfauts, caprettiez and flights; forward, backward, fydewize,

fydewize, a doownward, upward and with
fundry windings, gyrings & circumflexions;
allfo lightly and with fuch eazinefs, as by
mee in feaw words it is not expreffibl by pen
or fpeech I tell yoo plain. I bleaft me by
my faith to behold him, and began to doout
whither a waz a man or a fpirite, and I
ween had doouted mee 'till this day, had it
not been that anon I bethought me of men
that can reafon and talk with too toongs,
and with too parfons at onez, fing like Burdz,
curteiz of behaviour, of body ftrong, and in
joynts fo nymbl withall, that their bonez
feem az lythie and plyaunt fyneuz. They
dwel in a happy *Iland* (az the Book tearmz
it,) four moonths fayling Southward beyond
Ethiop. Nay *Mafter Martin* I tell you no
jeft; for both *Diodorus Siculus* an Auncient *Diodor. Sicul.*
Greek Hiftoriographer in his third book of $\frac{de\ Antig.}{Egyptiorum}$
the Acts of the olld *Egypcians;* and alfo from *Geftia. lib. 3.*
him *Conrad Gefnerus,* a great learned man,
and a very diligent Writer in all good Argu-
ments of oour time, but deceafed, in the
firft chapter of hiz *Mithridates* reporteth the
fame. As for this fellow, I cannot tell what
too make of him, fave that I may geffe his
bak metalld like a Lamprey, that haz no
bone, but a lyne like to a Lute ftring. Well
fyr,

fyr, let him paſs and his feats, and this dayz
paſtime withall, for heer iz az mooch az I
can remember mee for *Thurſdaiz* entertainment.

Friday, 7.
Saterday, 8. *Friday* and *Saterday* wear thear no open
ſheaws abrode, becauz the weather enclynde
too ſum moyſter and wynde; that very ſeaz-
onably temperd the drought and the heat,
cauzed by the continuans of fayr weather
and ſunſhyne afore, all the whyle ſyns her
Majeſtiez thither cumming.

Sunday, 9. A *Sunday,* opportunely the weather brake
up again, and after divine Servis in the
Pariſh Church for the Sabot day, and a
frutefull Sermon thear in the forenoon: At
Afternoon, in woorſhip of this *Kenelwoorth
Caſtl,* and of *God* and *Saint Kenelm,* whooz
day forſooth by the Calendar this waz; a
a Brideale. ſolemn Brydeale of a proper Coopl waz appointed; Set in order in the Tylt-yard, too
cum and make thear ſheaw before the *Caſtl*
in the great Coourt, whear az was pight a
cumly Quintine for featz at Armz, which
when they had done, too march oout at the
North gate of the *Caſtl* homeward again into the Tooun.

And

And thus were they marfhalld. Fyrft, all
the luftie Lads and bolld bachelarz of the
Parifh, futablie every Wight with hiz blu
buckeram bridelace upon a braunch of green
Broom (cauz rozemary iz fkant thear) tyed
on hiz leaft arme, (for a that fyde lyez the
heart,) and his Alder pole for a fpear in his
right hand, in Marciall order raungrd on a
fore, too and too in a rank: Sum with a
hat, fum in a Cap, fum a Cote, fum a jerken,
fum for lightnefs in hiz dooblet and hiz hoze,
Clean truft with a point afore: Sum botes
and no Spurz, he Spurz and no boots, and
he neyther nother: One a Sadel, anoother
a Pad or a Pannell faftened with a Cord, for
gyrts wear geazon: And theez to the number of a fixteen wight riding men and well
befeen: But the Bridegroom formoft, in
hiz fatherz tawny worfted jacket, (for hiz
freends wear fayn that he fhoold be a Brydegroom before the *Queen*) a fayr ftrawn hat
with a Capitall Crooun, fteepl Wyze on his
hed: a payr of harveft gloves on hiz hands,
az a fign of good Hufbandry: A Pen and
inkorn at hiz bak; for he woold be knowen
to be bookifh: lame of a leg that in his
Yooth was broken at football: Well beloved yet of his Mother, that lent him a nu Muf-
flar

flar for a Napkin that waz tyed too hiz gyrdl
for lozyng. It was no fmall Sport too marke
this Minion in hiz full apointment, that
throogh good fcoolation becam az formall
in hiz Action, az had he been a Brydegroom
indeed; with this fpeciall grace by the wey,
that ever az he woold have framed him the
better countenaùns, with the woors face he
lookt.

Well fyr, after theez horfmen, a lively
Morifdauns, according too the Auncient
manner: fix Dauncerz, Mawdmarion, and
the Fool. Then three pretty Puzels, az
bright az a breaft of bacon, of a thirtie yeere
old a pees, that carried three fpeciall Spife-
cakes óf a bufhel of wheat (they had it by
meazure out of my *Lords* backhoufe,) before
the Bryde: Syzely with fet countenauns,
and lips fo demurely fimpring, as it had been
a Mare cropping of a thiftl. After theez, a
loovely loober woorts, freklfaced, red-head-
ed, cleen truft in hiz dooblet and hiz hoze
taken up now in deed by commiffion, for
that hee waz fo loth to cum forward, for reverens belike of hiz nue cut-canvas dooblet;
and woold by hiz good will have been but a
gazer, but found to bee a meet actor for his
Offis:

Offis: That waz to beare the Bride-cup, foormed of a fweet fucket barrell, a faire turnd foot fet too it, all feemly be fylverd and parcell gilt, adourned with a beautiful braunch of Broom, gayly begilded for Rofe-mary; from which, too brode Brydelaces of red and yelloo buckeram begilded, and galauntly ftreaming by fuch wind az thear waz, for he Carried it aloft: This gentl Cup-bearer yet, had hiz freckld fiznemy fum-what unhappily infefted az he went, by the byzy flyez, that floſ about the Bride-cup, for the fweetnefs of the fucket that it favor-ed on: but hee like a tall Fello, withftood their Mallis ftoutly, (fee what Manhood may do,) bet them away, kild them by fcores, ftood to hiz charge, and marched on in good Order.

Then folloed the worfhipful Bride, led (after the Cuntrie maner) between too Auncient Parifhioners, honeft Toounfmen. But a ftale Stallion, and a well fpred, (hot az the Weather waz) God wot, and ill fmelling waz fhe: a thirtie yeer old, of colour broun-bay not very beautifull in deed, but ugly, and foul ill favord: Yet marvey-loous fond of the Offis, becaufe fhee hard

fay fhee fhoold dauns before the *Queen*, in
which feat fhee thought fhe woold foot it az
finely az the beft: Well, after this Bride
cam thear by too and too, a dozen damzels
for bride-maides; that for favor, attyre, for
facion and cleanlines, were az meete for fuch
a Bride az a treen ladl for a Porige Pot:
Mo, (but for fear of carring all clean,) had
been appointed but theez feaw wear inoow.

Runnins at
Quintine.

As the Cumpany in this Order wear cum
into the Coourt, marvelous wear the marcial
Aɛts that wear doon thear that day, The
Bryde-groome for preeminens had the fyrft
Coors at the Quintyne, brake hiz fpear
trefhardiment: but his Mare in hiz manage
did a littl fo titubate, that mooch a doo had
his Manhod to fit in his Sadl, and too 'fcape
the foyl of a fall: With the help of his
hand, yet hee recooverd himfelf, and loft
not hiz ftyrops (for he had none to his Sad-
dl:) had no hurt as it hapt, but only that
hiz gyrt burft, and loft hiz pen and inkorn
that he waz redy to wep for; but his hand-
kercher, az good hap waz, found hee fafe
at his gyrdl: that cheerd him fumwhat,
and had good regard it fhoold not be fyeld.
For though heat and coolnefs upon fundry
Occazions

Occazions made him fum time too fweat, and fum time rumatick; yet durft hee be bollder too blo his noze and wype his face with the flapet of his fatherz jacket, then with his Mother's Muffler: 'tis a goodly matter, when Yooth iz manerly brought up, in fatherlie loove and Motherly Aw.

Now Syr, after the Brydegroom had made hiz Coors, ran the reft of the Band a whyle, in fum order; but foon after, tag and rag, cut and long tail; whear the fpecialty of the fport was, to fee how fum for hiz flaknefs had a good bob with the Bag; and fum for his hafte too toppl dooun right, and cum tumbling to the Poft: Sum ftryving fo mooch at the fyrft fetting oout, that it feemd a queftion between the Man and the Beaft, whither the Coors fhoold be made a horfback or a foot: and put foorth with the fpurz, then wold run hiz race by az among the thickeft of the Throng, that dooun came they toogyther hand over hed: Anoother, whyle he directed his Coors to the quintine, his jument woold carry him too a Mare amoong the Pepl: So hiz hors az amoroos az him felf adventuroous: Another, too, run and mift the quintyne with

E   hiz

hiz ſtaff, and hit the boord with his hed!

Many ſuch gay gamz wear thear among
theez ryderz: who by and by after, upon a
greater coorage leaſt thear quintining, and
ran at anoother. Thear to ſee the ſtearn
countenauns, the grym looks, the coora-
gioous attempts, the deſperat Adventurez,
the daungeroous Coorvez, the feers encoounterz, whereby the buff at the Man,
and the counterbuff at the hors, that both
ſumtime cam topling to the ground. By my
trooth *Maſter Martyn* twaz a lively paſtime;
I beleeve it woold have mooved ſum man
too a right meerry mood, though had it be
toold him hiz Wife lay a dying.

Ilok Tuiſday by theCoventree men. And heerto folloed az good a ſport, (me-
thooght,) prezented in an Hiſtorical kue,
by certain good harted men of *Coventree*,
my Lords Neighboors thear: who under-
ſtanding amoong them the thing that coold
not bee hidden from ony: hoow carefull
and ſtudious hiz honour waz that by all
pleazaunt recreaſions her highnes might beſt
fynd her ſelf wellcom, and bee made glad-
ſum and mery; (the groundworke indeede
and foundacion of hiz Lordſhip's myrth and
gladneſſe

gladneſſe of us all,) made petition that they
moought renue noow their Old Storial
Sheaw: Of argument how the *Danez* why-
lom heere in a troubloous Seazon wear for
quietneſſe born withall and ſuffeard in Peaſ;
that anon, by outrage and importabl in-
ſolency, abuzing both *Ethelred* the *King*,
then, and all Eſtates everie whear by ſyde;
at the greevous complaint and coounſel of
Huna the *King's* Chieftain in warz, on *Saint*
Brice's night, *Ann. Dom.* 1012, (az the book
ſayz, that falleth yeerely on the thirteenth of
November) wear all diſpatcht and the Ream
rid. And for becauz the matter mencioneth
how valiantly our *Engliſh* Women, for love
of their Countree behaved themſelves, ex-
preſſed in Actionz and rymez after their
manner, they thought it moought moove
ſum myrth to her *Majeſty* the rather. The
thing, ſaid They, iz grounded in ſtory, and
for paſtime woont too be plaid in oour Citee
yearly: without ill example of mannerz,
papiſtry, on ony ſuperſtition: and elz did ſo
occupy the heads of a number, that likely
inoough woold have had woorz meditationz:
had an Auncient beginning and a long continuauns: 'till noow of late laid dooun, they
knue no cauz why, onleſs it wear by the

zeal

zeal of certain theyr preacherz; Men very
commendabl for their behaviour & learning,
and fweet in their Sermons, but fumwhat
too four in preaching awey theyr Paftime:
Wifht therefore, that az they fhoold continue
their good doctrine in Pulpet, fo, for matters of pollicy and governauns of the Citie,
they woold permit them to the *Mair* and
Magiftratez: and fayed by my feyth, *Mafter*
Martyn, they woold make theyr humbl peti-
cion untoo her highnes, that they might have
theyr Playz up agayn.

But aware, keep bak, make room noow,
har they cum:

Captain Cox. And fyrft *Captin Cox*, an od man I pro-
miz yoo: by profeffion a Mafon, and that
It is alluding to
this Adventure right fkilfull; very cunning in fens, and
of the Country
men, that Ben. hardy as *Gawin;* for his ton-fword hangs at
Johnfon names hiz tablz eend: great overfight hath he in mat-
one of his Maf-
ques,which was ters of ftorie: For az for *King Arthurz* Book,
printed 1640;
A Mafques of *Huon* of *Burdeaus,* the foour fons of *Aymon,*
Owls at Kenel- *Bevys* of *Hampton,* The *Squyre* of lo degree,
worth; prefent-
ed by the Ghoft The *Knight* of *Courtefy,* and the *Lady Fagu-*
of Captain Cox,
mounted on his *ell,* *Frederik* of *Gene,* *Syr Eglamoour,* *Syr*
Hobbyhorfe.
See Langbain's *Tryamoour, Syr Lamwell, Syr Ifenbras, Syr*
Dramatic Poets *Gawyn,* *Olyver* of the *Caftl, Lucres* and
p. 293.
J. C. *Eurialus, Virgil's life,* the *Cuftl* of *Ladies,*
the

the *Wido Edyth*, the *King* and the *Tanner*,
Frier Rous, *Howleglas*, *Gargantua*, *Robin-
hood*, *Adam Bel*, *Clim* of the *Clough* and
William of *Cloudſley*, the *Churl* & the *Burd*,
the *ſeaven wiſe Maſters*, the *Wiſe* lapt in a
Morels ſkin, the *ſak full of Nucz*, the *Searge-
aunt* that became a *Fryar*, *Skogan*, *Collyn
Cloout*, the *Fryar* and the *boy*, *Elynor-Rumm-
ing*, and the *Nutbrooun Maid*, with many moe
then I rehears heere; I beleeve hee have them
all at his fingers endz.

Then in Philoſophy, both Morall and
Naturall, I think hee be as naturally over-
ſeen; beſide *Poetrie* and *Aſtronomie*, and
oother hid *Sciences*, az I may geſſe by the
Omberty of his Books; whearof part, az I
remember, The *Sheperds Kalendar*, The
Ship of *Fools*, *Danielz Dreamz*, the *Book* of
Fortune, *Stans puer ad Menſam*, The bye
wey to the *Spitl-houſe*, *Julian of Brainford's
Teſtament*, the *Caſtle* of *Love*, the *Booget* of
Demaunds, the *Hundred Mery Talez*, the
Book of Riddels, the *Seaven Sororz* of *Wemen*,
The *prooud Wives Pater-Noſter*, the *Chapman*
of a *Peniwoorth* of *Wit:* Beſide hiz Auncient
Playz, *Yooth* & *Charitee*, *Hikſkorner*, *Nugize*,
Impacient Poverty, & heerwith *Doctor Boords
Breviary*

Breviary of *Health.* What fhoold I rehearz
:heer, what a bunch of Ballets and Songs,
all Auncient; as *Broum broom* on *Hil, So
Wo iz me begon, trolly lo. Over a Whinny
Meg, Hey ding a ding, Bony lafs upon a
green, My bony on gave me a bek. By a bank
az I lay:* and too more he hath fair wrapt
up in Parchment, and bound with a Whip-
cord. And az for Almanaks of Antiquitee,
(a point for *Ephemerides*) I ween he can
fheaw from *Jafper Laet* of *Antwarp* unto
Noftradam of *Frauns,* and thens untoo oour
John Securiz of *Salfbury.* To ftay ye no
longer herein, I dare fay hee hath az fair a
Library of theez Sciencez, and az many
goodly Monuments both in Proze and Poe-
try, and at afternoonz can talk az much
without book, az ony Inholder betwixt
Brainford and *Bagfhot,* what degree foever
he be.

Befide thiz, in the field a good Marfhall
at mufters; of very great Credite and truft
in the Toun here; for he haz been chozen
Ale-cunner many a Yeer, when hiz betterz
have ftond by; and ever quited himfelf with
fuch eftimation, az yet too taft of a Cup of
Nippitate, hiz judgement will be taken a-
bove

bove the beſt in the Pariſh, be hiz noze near
ſo read.

Captain Cox cam marching on valiantly
before, cleen truſt and gartered above the
knee, all freſh in a Velvet Cap *(Maſter Gold-*
ing a lent it him,) flooriſhing with hiz ton
ſwoord; and another fens maſter with him:
Thus in the forward making room for the
reſt. After them, proudly prickt on for-
moſt the *Daniſh* launce knights on hoſbak,
and then the *Engliſh:* Each with their Al-
der pole martially in their hand. Eeven at *The Coventree*
the firſt entree, the meeting waxt ſum-what *Play.*
Warm; that bye and bye kindled with corage
a both ſidez, grue from a hot ſkirmiſh unto
a blazing Battail: firſt by ſpeare and ſhield,
outragious in their racez as ramz at their rut;
with furious encoounterz, that togyther they
tumbl too the duſt, ſumtime hors and man,
and after ſall too it with ſworde and target,
good bangz a both ſidez. The fight ſo
ceaſing, but the Battail not ſo ended folloed the Footmen: both by the Hoſtes ton a-
fter toother; firſt marching in ranks; then
Warlik turning; then fro ranks into ſquad-
rons; then intoo triangles; fro that into
rings, and ſo winding oout again. A valiant
Captain

Captain of great prowez az fiers az a fox affauting a gooz, waz fo hardy to give the firft ftroke: then get they gryfly togyther, that great was the Activitee that day too befeen thear a both fidez: ton very eager for purchaz of pray, toother utterly ftoout for redemption of Libertie: thus, quarrell enflamed fury a both fidez: Twife the *Danes* had the better, but at the laft conflict, beaten doun, overcom, and many led captive for triumph by our *Englifh* Weemen.

This was the effect of this Sheaw; that az it waz handled, made mooch matter of good Paftime: brought all indeed into the great Coourt, een under her highnes windo too have feen: but (az unhappy it waz for the Bride) that cam thither too foon, (and yet waz it a four a Clok.) for her highnes beholding in the Chamber delectabl daucing indeed, and heerwith the great throng and unrulinefs of the people, waz cauz that this folemnitee of Brideale and daucing, had not the full mufter was hoped for; and but a littl of the *Coventree* Pley her highnes alfo faw, commaunded therefore on the *Tuifday* folloing to have it full oout: az accordingly it waz prezented; whereat.
                                                her

her *Majefty* laught well: They wear the Jocunder, and fo mooch the more, becauz her highnes had given them too Buckes and five Marke in mony, to make mery to-gyther: They prayed for her *Majefty*, long, happily to reign, and oft to cum thither, that oft they moought fee her: and what, triumphing upon the good acceptauns, they vaunted their Play was never fo dignified, nor ever any Players before fo beatified.

Thus, tho' the Day took an end, yet flipt not the night all fleeping awey: for az ney-ther Offis not obfequie ceaffed at any time too the full; to perform the Plot his Honor had appoynted: So after fupper waz thear a Play of a very good Theam prefented, but fo fet foorth, by the Actours well handling, that pleazure and mirth made it feem very fhort, tho' it lafted too good oourz & more. But ftay *Mafter Martyn*, all iz not doon yet.

After the Play, oout of hand folloed a moft delicioous and (if I may fo terme it) an Ambrofiall Banket: whearof, whither I might more muze at the deintyneffe, fhapez, and the coft; or elfe at the variete and num-

ber

ber of the difhes (that wear a three hundred)
for my part I coold littl tell them; and now
lefs I affure yoo. Her *Majefty* eat fmally or
nothing: which underftood; the Coorfez
wear not fo Orderly ferved and fizely fet
dooud, but wear by and by as diforderly
wafted and coorfly confumed;. more courtly
me thought than curteoufly: But that was
no part of the matter; moought it pleaz and
be liked, and do that it cam for, then was all
well inough.

Untoo this Banket thear was appoynted
a Malk: for riches of Aray, of an incredibl
coft:. but the time fo far fpent, and very
late in the night now, was cauz that it cam
not foorth to the fheaw: And thus for *Son-
dayz* feafon, having ftayd yoo the longer,
according to the matter, heer make I an
eend: Ye maye breath yee a while.

Munday the eyghteenth of this *July,* the
Weather being hot, her highnes kept the
Caftl for coolnefs, 'till about five a Clok, her
Majefty in the Chafe hunted the Hart (as a-
fore) of fors: that whyther wear it by the
cunning of the Huntfmen, or by the natural
defyre of the Deer, or els by both; anon he
gat

gat him to foyl agayne, which reyzed the accuftomed delight: a Paftime indeede fo intyrely pleazaunt, az whearof at times whoo may have the full and free fruition, can find no more facietee (I ween) for a Recreation, then of theyr good Viaundes at timez for their fuftentation.

Well, the Game was gotten; and her Highnes returning, cam thear, upon a fwimming Mermayd, (that from top too tayl waz an eyghteen foot long,) *Triton Neptune's* blafter: whoo, with his Trumpet foormed of a Wrinkld Wealk, az her *Majefty* waz in fight, gave foound very fhrill & fonoroous, in fign he had an Ambaffy too pronoouns. Anon her highnes was cummen upon the bridge, whearunto he made hiz Fifh to fwim the fwifter; and he then declared——"How
" the fupreame falfipotent Monarch *Neptune*,
" the great *God* of the fwelling Seas, Prins
" of Profunditees, and Sooverain Segnior of
" al Lakez, frefh Waterz, Riverz, Creekez
" and Goolphs; Underftanding how a cruel
" *Knight*, one *Syr Bruce Sans Pitee*, a mor-
" tal Enemy untoo *Ladiz* of eftate; had
" long lien about the banks of this Pool in
" wayt with his bands, heer to diftrefs the
" *Lady*

" *Lady* of the *Lake*, whearby fhe hath been
" reftrayned not only from having any ufe of
" her Ancient Liberty & territoriez in theeze
" parts; but alfo of making repayr and giving
" attendauns unto yoo Nobl *Queen* (quo' he)
" az fhe woold; fhe promift, and alfo fhoold;
" dooth therefoer fignify, and heerto, of yoo
" az of his good Leag and deer freend make
" this Requeft, that ye will deyn but too
" fheaw yoor Parfon toward this Pool;
" whearby yoor only prezens fhall be mat-
" ter fufficient of abandoning this uncurtefs
" *Knight*, and putting all his Bands too
" flight, and alfo deliveraunce of the *Lady*
" oout of this thralldom."

Mooving heerwith from the Bridge, and
fleeting more into the Pool, chargeth he in
Neptune's name both *Eolus* with all his
Windez, the Waterz with his Springez, his
Fyfh and Fooul, and all his Clients in the
fame, that they ne be fo hardye in any fors
to ftur, but keep them Calm and quiet while
this *Queen* be prezent. At which petition,
her Highnefs ftaying, it appeerd ftraight
hoow *Syr Bruce* became unfeen, his Bands
fkaled, and the *Lady* by and by, with her
two *Nymphs* floating upon her moovable

Ilands

Ilands (*Triton* on his Mermaid fkimming by,) approched toward her highnes on the Bridge;———as well too declare that her *Majefiez* prezens hath fo graciouflie thus wrought her deliverauns, az allfo to excuze her not comming to Coourt az fhe promift, and cheefly to prezent her *Majeftie* (as a token of her Duty and good hart) for her highnefs recreation, with this Gift; which was *Arion* that excellent and famous Muzicien, in tyre and appointment ftraunge well feeming too his Parfon, ryding alofte upon his old freend the Dolphin, (that from hed too tayl waz a foour and twenty foot long,) and fwymd hard by theez *Ilands.* Heerwith, *Arion*, for theez great Benefitez, after a feaw well coouched woords unto her *Majefty* of thankfgiving, in fupplement of the fame; began a delectabl Ditty of a Song well apted to a melodious noiz; compoounded of fix feveral Inftruments, all covert, cafting foound from the Dolphin's belly within; *Arion*, the feaventh, fitting thus finging (az I fay) without.

Noow Syr, the Ditty in meeter fo aptly endighted to the matter, and after by Voys fo delicioously deliver'd; The Song, by a

fkilfull

ſkilfull Artiſt into hiz parts ſo ſweetlie ſorted; each part in his Inſtrument ſo clean and
ſharpely touched; Every Inſtrument agayn
in hiz kind ſo excellently tunabl; and this.
in the Eeving of the day, reſoounding from
the Calmm Waters, whear prezens of her
Majeſty, and longing to liſten had utterly
damped all noiz and din; the whole Armony
conveyd in tyme tune and temper thus in-
comparably Melodious; with what pleazure
(Maſter Martyn) with what ſharpneſs of
Conceyt, with what lively delighte this
mought pearce into the hearers harts; I
pray ye imagin yoor ſelf az ye may; for ſo
God judge me, by all the Wit and Cunning
I have, I cannot expreſs, I promis yoo.
" Mais ieo bien vieu cela Monſieur, que
" forte grande eſt la pouvoyr qu' avoit la
" tres nobl Science de Muſique ſur les eſprites
" humains. Perceive ye me? I have told
ye a great matter noow: As for me, ſure-
ly I was lull'd in ſuch liking, and ſo loth too
leave off, that mooch a doo a good while
after, had I, to fynde me whear I waz.
And take ye this by the way, that for the
ſmall Skyl in Muzik, that *God* hath ſent
me (ye kno it iz ſumwhat) ile ſet the more
by my ſelf while my name is *Laneham*;
and

and Grace a *God*, a Muzik iz a Nobl Art!

A, ftay a while, fee a fhort wit: by trooth *Knights madc.*
I had almoft forgot. This daye waz a day
of Grace befide, whearin wear avaunced
five Gentlemen of woorfhippe unto the degree of *Knighthood; Sir Thomas Cecyl*, fun
and heyr untoo the right honorabl the *Lord
Treazorer, Syr Henry Cobham*, broother unto the *Lord Cobham, Syr Thomas Stanhop,
Syr Arthur Baffet*, and *Syr Thomas Trefham*.
and alfo, by her highnes accuftumed mercy
and charitee, nyne cured of the peynfull and
daungerous defeaz called the *King's Evill;*
for that *Kings* and *Queens* of this *Realm*,
withoout oother medfin (fave only by handling prayerz) only doo cure it: Bear with
me, tho' perchaunce I place not thoz Gentlmen in my recitall heer, after theyr eftatez;
for I am neyther good Heraud of Armes,
nor yet kno hoow they are fet in the Subfidy
bookez: men of great woorfhip I under-
ftand they are all.

Tuifday, according to commaundement, *Tuifday*, 11.
cam oour *Coventree* men. What their matter was, of her highnes myrth and good acceptauns, and Rewarde untoo them, and
of

of their rejoyfing thearat, I fheawd you a-
fore, and fo fay the lefs noow.

Wednefd. 12. *Wednefday* in the forenoon, preparacion
was in hand for her *Majefty* to have fupt in
Now call'd *Wedgenall,* a three Myle weft from the *Caftl.*
Wedgnockpark.
J. G. A goodly Park of the *Queenz Majeftiez:*
For that cauz a fair pavilion, and other pro-
vifion accordingly thither fent and prepared:
but by meanz of Weather not fo cleerly dif-
pozed, the matter waz countermaunded a-
gain: That had her highnes hapned this
daye too have cummen abrode, there was
made reddy a Devife of *Godeffez* & *Nymphes;*
which az well for the ingenious argument,
az for the well handling of it in rime and en-
dighting, woold undooutedly have gaind
great lyking and mooved no lefs delight:
Of the Particulariteez whearof I ceas to en-
treat, leaft like the boongling Carpentar;
by mifforting the peecez, I mar a good frame
in the bad fetting up; or by my bad tempring afore hand, embleamifhe the beauty, when
it fhoold be rear'd up indeed. A This Day
allfo waz thear fuch earneft tallk and appointment of remooving, that I gave over
my Noteing, and harkened after my hors.

Mary

Mary fyr, I muſt tell yoo; Az all en-
deavoour waz to moove mirth and Paſtime
(az I tolld ye:) Eeven ſo a ridiculoous De-
viſe of an Auncient Minſtrell and his Song, *The Minſtrel.*
waz prepared to have been proffer'd, if meete
time and place had been foound for it. Ons,
in a woorſhipful Company, whear, full appointed, he recoounted his matter in ſort az
it ſhould have been uttered, I chaunſed to
bee; what I noted, heer thus I tell yoo.

A Parſon very meet ſeemed he for the purpoze; of a XLV years olld, apparelled partly as he woold himſelf: Hiz Cap of hiz hed
ſeemly rounded tonſter wyze; fayr kembd,
that with a ſpoonge deintly dipt in a littl
Caponz greas, waz finelye ſmoothed too
make it ſhine like a Mallards wing. hiz
beard ſmugly ſhaven; and yet his ſhyrt after
the nu trink, with ruffs fayr ſtarched, ſleek-
ed, and gliſtering like a payr of nu ſhooz:
Marſhalld in good Order: wyth a ſtetting
ſtick, and ſtoout that every ruff ſtood up
like a wafer. A ſide gooun of Kendal green,
after the freſhneſs of the year now; gathered at the Neck with a narro gorget faſtened
afore with a white claſp and a keepar cloſe
up to the Chin, but eaſily for heat too un-
G   doo

doo when he lift: feemly begyrt in a red
Caddíz gyrdl; from that, a payr of capped
Sheffeld knivez hanging a to fide: Out of
hiz bozom draune foorth a lappet of his Napkin, edged with a blu lace, and marked with
a truloove, a hart, and *A. D.* for *Damian:*
for he was but a bachelar yet:

His gooun had fyde fleevez dooun to mid-
legge, flit from the fhooulder too the hand;
and lined with white Cotten. His dooblet
fleevez of blak woorfted; upon them a payr
of poynets of tawny Chamblet, laced a long
the wreaft wyth blu threeden points; a wealt
toward the hand of fuftian anapes: a payr
of red neather- ftocks: a payr of Pumps
on hiz feet, with a Crofs cut at the toze for
Cornz; not nu indeede, yet cleanly blakt
with foot, and fhining az a fhoing horn. A-
boout hiz Neck, a red rebond futabl to his
girdl: His Harp in good grace dependaunt be-
a Wreaft, is fore him; his wreaft tyed to a green lace and
a Tuncing ham-
mer, or turn- hanging by: Under the gorget of his goound
Scrue.
a fayr flagon cheyn of Pewter, (for Sylver;)
as a *Squire Minftrel* of *Middilfex*, that tra-
vaild the Cuntree thys foomer feafon unto
Fayrz, and woorfhipfull menz houzez. From
hiz cheyn hoong a Schoochion, with met-
all

all and cooller refplendant upon hiz breaft,
of the auncient Armes of *Iflington:* Upon
a queftion whearof, he, az one that waz well
School'd, & coold his leffon parfit withoout
booke too aunfwear at full, if queftion wear
afkt hym, declared: "How the woorfhip-
" full Village of *Iflington* in *Middelfex*, well
" knoen too bee one of the moft auncient
" and beft Toouns in *England* next *London*
" at thiz day; for the feythfull freendfhip of
" long time fheawed, az well at *Cookez* feaft
" in *Alderfgate-ftreete* yeerely upon *Holly*
" *Rood day*, az allfo at all folem Bridealez
" in the Citie of *London* all the yeer after;
" in well ferving them of furmenty for por-
" age, not overfod till it be too weak: of
" Mylk for theyr flawnez, not pild nor chalk-
" ed; of Cream for their Cuftardes, not froth-
" ed nor thykned with floour: and of But-
" ter for their Paftiez and Pye-pafte, not
" made of well Curds, nor gatherd of Whey
" in foommer, nor mingled in Winter with
" falt-butter watered or wafht; did obteyn
" long ago thez Woorfhipfull Armez in
" cooler and foorm az yee fee: which are
" The Arms, A field Argent, as the field and
" groound indeed whearin the Milk-wives
" of this woorthy Tooun, and every man

Iflington Arms.

G 2   " els

" els in his faculty, doth trade for his liv-
" ing. On a fefs tenny three Platez between
" three Milke tankerds proper. The three
" Milk Tankerds, az the proper Veffell
" whearin the fubftaunce and matter of their
" trade is too and fro tranfported. The
" fefs tenny, which iz a cooler betokening
" dout and fufpition; fo az fufpition and
" good heed taking, as wel to their Markets
" and Servants, as to their Cuftomerz that
" they truft not too farre; may bring unto
" them Platez, that iz Coynnd Sylver; three,
" that iz fufficient and plentie; for fo that
" Number in Armory may well fignifie.

The horn-fpoons.

" For Creaft, upon a Wad of Ote ftrawe
" for a Wreath, a boll of furmenty: Wheat
" (az ye kno) iz the moft precious Gift of
" Ceres; and in the midft of it fticking, a
" doozen of horn-fpoonz in a bunch, az the
" Inftruments meeteft too eate furmenty por-
" age wythall: a doozen, az a number of
" plenty compleat for full cheere or a Ban-
" ket; and of Horn, az of a fubftauns more
" eftimabl then iz made for a great deel;
" beeing nether fo churlifh in weight, az
" iz mettal; nor fo froward and brittl to
" manure, as ftone; nor yet fo foily in ufe
" nor

" nor roough to the lips, as wood is; but
" lyght, pliaunt, and fmooth; that with a
" littl licking, wool alweyz be kept az
" clen az a dye. With yoor paciens *Gentle-*
" *men* (quoth the Minftrel) be it faid; wear
" it not in deede that hornz bee fo plentie,
" Hornware, I beleeve woold bee more fet
" by than it iz; and yet ther arr in our parts
" that wyl not ftick too avow, that many an
" honeft man, both in Citee & Cuntree, hath
" had his hooufe by horning well upholden,
" and a daily freend allfo at need: And
" this with your favoour may I further
" affirm; a very ingenious Parfon waz hee,
" that for dignittee of the ftuff, coold thus by
" fpooning devife to advauns the horn fo
" neer to the Head. With great congruens
" alfo wear theez horn-fpoonz put too the
" Wheat; az a token and porcion of *Cornu-* *Ovid. Metai-*
" *copiæ*, the horn of *Achelous;* which the   *morph. Lib. 9.*
" Maiades did fill with all good frutez, Corn
" and Grain; and after did confecrate unto
" aboundauns and plenty.

" This Shoochion with Beaftz, very aptly
" agreeing both to the Arms, and to the trade
" of the bearers; gloriooufly fupported. Be-
" tween a gray Mare, (a beaft meeteft for
                                    "carying

" carying of Milk tankards) her pannell on
" her bak, az alwaies reddy for fervis at
" every Feaft and Brideale at neede; her
" tayl fplayd at moft eaz; and her filly fole,
" fallow and flaxen mane after the fyre.

" In the fkro under-graven (quoth hee) iz
" thear a proper woord, an *Hemiftichi*, well
" fquaring with ail the reft, taken out of
" *Salerns* chapter, of things that mooft
Schola Salerni. " noorifh mans Body: Lac, Cafeus infans.
" That iz, Good Milk, and young cheez.
" And thus mooch, *Gentlmen*, and pleaz you
" (quoth he) for the Armz of oour Woorfhip-
" ful Tooun:" and thearwithall made a
manerly leg, and fo held hiz Peafe.

Az the Cumpany pawzed, and the Minftrel feemde to gape after a praiz for hiz
Beau parlea: and bicauz he had renderd
hiz leffon fo well: Saiz a good fello of the
Cumpany, "I am fory to fee how mooch
" the poore Minftrel miftakes the matter;
" for indeed the Armez are thus:

" Three Milk tankerds proper, in a fielde
" of cloouted Cream, three green cheefez
" upon a fhealf of Cake-bread. The Fyr-
" menty

" menty boll and horn fpoonz: cauz their
" profit coms all by horned Beafts. Support-
" ed by a Mare with a gald back, and thear-
" fore ftill cooverd with a panniell, fifking
" with her tail for flyez, and her filly Fole
" neying after the Dam for fuk. This woord
" *Lac, Cafeus infans,* that iz, a frefh Cheez
" and Cream, and the common cry that
" theeze Milk-wives make in *London* ftreets
" yeerly betwixt *Eafter* and *Whitfontide:*
" and this iz the very matter I kno it well
" enough: and fo ended hiz Tale and fate
" him dooun again."

Heerat every man laught a good, fave the
Minftrell: that thoogh the fooll wear made
privy, all waz but for fport, yet too fee himfelf thus croft with a contrary kue that hee
lookt not for, woold ftraight have ge'en
over all; waxt very wayward, eager and
foour: hoowbeit at lafte, by fum entreaty,
and many fair woordz, with fak and fuger,
we fweetned him againe: and after he becam az mery az a Py. Appeerez then a
frefh, in hiz ful formalitee with a lovely
loock: After three lowlie coourfiez, cleer-
ed his vois with a hem and reach, and fpat
oout withal; wiped hiz lips with the hollo

of

of his hand, for fyling hiz napkin, temperd
a ftring or too with his wreaft, and after a
littl warbling on hiz Harp for a prelude,
came foorth with a Sollem Song, warraunt-
King Arthurs
Book. ed for ftory oout of *King Arthur's* Acts; The
firft booke, and 26 Chapter; whearof I gate
a Copy: And that iz this: viz.

[*The Minftrell's Sonnett.*]

So it befell upon a Pentecoft day,
When *King Arthur* at Camelot kept Coourt rial,
With his cumly *Queen* dame Gaynoour the gay,
And many bolld Barons fitting in hall;
Ladies apparaild in Purpl and Pall.
When Herauds in hukes herried full by
Largefs Largefs Chevaliers trefhardy.

A doouty Dwarf too the uppermoft deas
Right peartly gan prik, and kneeling on knee,
With fteeven full ftoout amids all the preas,
Said hail *Syr King, God* thee fave and fee;
King Ryens of *Northgalez* greeteth well thee,
And bids that thy beard anon thou him fend,
Or els from thy jawz he will it of rend.

For his robe of ftate, a rich fkarlet mantell,
With a leaven *Kings* beards bordred aboout,
He hath made late, and yet in a cantell

Iz leaſt a place the twelth to make oout,
Whear thien muſt ſtand bee thou never ſo ſtoout;
This muſt bee doon I tell thee no fabl,
Mawgre the poour of all thy round tabl.

When this mortal Meſſage from hiz mouth waz paſt,
Great waz the brute in Hall and in Boour,
The *King* fumed, the *Queen* ſhriked, *Ladiez* wear agaſt,
Princes puſt, *Barnz* bluſtered, *Lordz* began too loour,
Knightz ſtampt, *Squirez* ſtartld az ſteedz in a ſtoour.
Yeemen and *Pages* yeald oout in the Hall,
Thearwith cam in *Syr Kay* of *Seneſhall*.

Sylens my ſuffrainz quoth the courteyz *Knight*.
And in that ſtoound the chearm becam ſtill,
The *Dwaſs* dynner full deerly waz dight,
For wine and waſtell hee had at hiz will;
And when he had eaten and fed hiz fill,
One hundred peeces of coyned gould,
Wear given the *Dwarf* for hiz meſſage bolld.

Say too *Syr Ryens* thou *Dwarf* quoth the *King*,
That for his proud meſſage I him defy,
And ſhortly with baſins and panz will him ring
Oout of *Northgalez*, whearaz hee and I
With Sweards and no razerz ſhall utterly try
Which of us both iz the better Barber:
And thearwith, he ſhook hiz ſword *Excalaber*!

H   At

At this the Minftrell made a pauz and a
curtezy, for primus paftus. More of the
Song iz thear, but I gat it not. Az for the
matter, had it cum to the Sheaw, I think the
Fello would have handled it well ynoough.

Her Highnefs tarryed at *Kyllingwoorth*
tyll the *Wednefday* after, being the 27 of this
July, and the *Ninteenth* (inclufive) of her
Majeftiez cumming thither. For which feven
daiz, perceyving my notez fo flenderly
aunfwering, I tooke it lefs blame too ceas,
and thearof to write yoo nothing at al, then
in fuch matterz to write nothing likely:
And fo mooch the rather, (az I have well
bethooght me) that if I dyd but ruminate
the dayz I have fpoken of, I fhall bring oout
yet fumwhat moor meet for yoor appetite,
(thoogh a deinty tooth have ye) which I be-
leve yoor tender ftomach will brook well
inoogh.

The Seavens. Whearof part iz fyrft hoow according to
her highnes name *Elizabeth*, which I heer
fay oout of the Hebru fignifieth (amoong
ɔother) the *Seaventh of my God:* diverz
things heer, did foo juftly in number fquare
with the fame. Az fyrft, her highnefs hither
cumming

cumming in this feaventh moonth: then, prezented with the feaven Prezents of the Seaven *Gods:* And after, with the Melody of the feaven forted Muzik in the Dollphin, the Lake-Ladiez gyft. Then too confider, how fully the *Gods* (az it feemed) had confpyred moft magnificently in aboundauns too beftow theyr influencez and gyfts upon her coourt thear to make her *Majefty* merry.

Sage *Saturn* himfelf in parfon (that by-cauz of hiz lame leg coold not fo well ftur) in chayr thearfore too take order with the grave Officerz of Houfehold, holpen indeed with the good advife of hiz prudent Nees *Pallas:* That no unruly body or difquiet difturb the nobl affemblee, or els be ons fo bolld too enter within the *Caftl* gatez. Awey with all rafcalls, captivez, melancholik, waiward, froward, Conjurerz, and Ufurers, and to have laborers and underwoork men for the beautifying of oney place, alwey at hand az they fhoold be commaunded.

Jupiter fent Parfonages of hy honor and dignitee: *Barons, Lords, Ladies, Juges, Bifhops, Lawyerz, Doctors:* With them, Vertu, Noblnefs, equitee, Liberalitee, and compaffion;

Saturn, and Pallas.

Jupiter.

H2

compaffion: due Seazon, and fayr weather:
faving that at the petition of hiz deer fifter
Ceres, he graunted a day or two of fum fweet
fhoourz, for rypening of her Corn that waz
fo well fet, and too fet forward Harveft.
Heerwith, beftoed he fuch plenty of pleazaunt
Thunder, Lightning, and thunderbolts, by
his halting fun and fyermafter *Vulcan*, ftill
frefh and frefh framed: alweyz fo frequent,
fo intellabl, and of fuch continuauns in the
fpending (az I partly tolld ye) confumed,
that furely he feemz to be az of Poor in-
eftimabl: fo, in ftore of municion, unwaftabl;
for all *Ovid's* cenfure, that faiz

Si quoties peccant homines fua fulmina mittat
Jupiter, exiguo tempore inermis erit.
If *Jove* fhoold fhoot his Thunderbolts az oft az men offend,
Affure you iz Artillary wold foon be at at an end!

What a number of Eftatez and of Nobilitee
had *Jupiter* affembled thear, gefs ye by thys,
that of fort woorfhipfull thear wear in the
coourt dayly aboove fourty, whearof the
meyeneft, of a thouzand mark yeerly revenu,
and many of mooch more. This great gyft
byfide, did hiz deitee caft upon her highnes,
too have fayr and feazonabl weather at her
ooun appointment; According whearunto
her *Majefty* fo had. For her gracious prezens thearfore with this great gift indewed,
Lichfeeld,

Lichfeeld, Worceter, and *Middelton,* with manye places mo, made humbl fute untoo her hignes too cum: too fuch whearof az her *Majefty* coold, it cam, and they feazon acceptabl.

Phœbus, bifide his continuall and moft delicious Muzik, (az I have toold yoo) appointed he Princes too adourn her highnes Coourt, Coounfelerz, Herauds, and fanguine Youth, pleazaunt & mery, coftlye garments, learned Phizicianz, and no need of them.

Juno, Golld Cheynez, Ouchez, Jewels of gret price and rich attire, woorn in mooch grace, and good befeeming, without pryde, or emulacion of ony.

Mars, Captainz of good Conduɛt, Men fkylfull in feats of Armz, pollitik in ftratagems, good Coorage in good Quarelz, Valiant and Wizehardy: abandoning pikquarrells and ruffians: appoynting alfo purfyvaunts, Currars, and Pofts, ftill feeding her highnes with Nuze and intelligencez from all parts.

Venus, Untoo the Ladiez & Gentlwemen, Beauty, good favor, Cumlinefs, galant attyre, dauncing with cumly grace, fweet vois in fong & pleazaunt talk, with exprefs commaundment and charge untoo her funn on

her

Phœbu.

Juno.

Mars.

Venus.

her Bleffing, that he fhoot not a fhaft in the Coourt all the while her highnes remayned at *Killingwoorth*.

Mercuri.   *Mercury,* Learned men in Sciences, Poets, Merchaunts, Painterz, Karverz, Playerz, Engynerz, Devyferz, and dexteritee in handling of all pleazaunt attempts.

Luna.   *Luna,* Callm nights for quiet reft, and fylver moonfhine, that nightly in deed fhone for moft of her *Majefliez* beeing thear.

Plutus.   Blind *Plutus,* Bags of Moony, Cuftumerz, Exchaungers, Bankers, ftore of riches in Plate and in Coyn.

Bacchus.   *Bacchus,* Full Cups every whear, every oour, of all Kynds of Wyne. Thear waz no deintee that the Sea coold yeeld, but

Neptune.   *Neptune* (thoough his Reign at the neereft ly well ny a hundred mile of) did dayly fend in great plenty, fweet and freafh. As for freafh-water fifh, the ftore of all forts waz aboundaunt.

Ceres.   And hoow bountifull *Ceres* in provizion waz, gefs ye by this, that in lytel more then a three dayz fpace, 72 tunn of Ale and Beer was pyept up quite: what that mighte whilft with it of Bread befide Meat, I report me to yoo: and yet *Mafter Controller, Mafter Coferar,* and diverz Officers of the Coourt,

fum

fum honorabl, and fundrye right woorfhipfull placed at *Warwik*, for more rooum in
the *Caftl*. But heer waz no ho *Mafter Martin*
in devoout drinking allwey; that brought
lak unlookt for; whiche being knoen too the
Woorfhipfull my *Lords* good Neighboorz,
cam thear in a too dayz fpace, from fundry
friendz, a releef of a XL Tunn, 'till a nu
fupply waz gotten agayn: and then too oour
drinking a frefhe az faft az ever we did.

Flora, Abrode and within the hooufe, *Flora.*
miniftred of Flourz fo great a quantitee, of
fuch fweet Savoour, fo beautifully hued,
fo large and fayr proporcion, and of fo
ftraunge kindez and fhapez, that it waz
great pleafure too fee: and fo mooch the
more, az thear waz great ftore yet counterfet,
and foormed of featherz by Art; lyke glorioous too the fheaw az wear the naturall.

Portheus, Hiz Tumbler that coold by *Protheu-*
nimblnefs caft himfelf into fo many foorms
and facionz.

Pan, His merry morrys dauns with theyr *Pan.*
Pype and taber.

Bellona, Her Quintine knights, and pro- *Bellona.*
per Bickerings of the *Coventree* men.

Polyphemus, *Neptunez* fun and heyr: (let *Polyphemus.*
him I pray, and if it be but for his father's
fake

fake, and for hiz good will, be allowed for a *God,*) with his Bearz, his Bearwhealps and Bandogs.

Æolus.   *Æolus,* Holding up hiz Windz, while her Highnes at any tyme took pleazure on the Water, and ftaying of Tempefts during a-bode heer.

Sylvanus.   *Sylvanus,* Befide hiz plentifull provizion of fooul for deynty Viaunds, his pleazaunt and fweet finging Byrds: whearof I will fheaw yoo more anon.

Echo.   *Echo,* Her well endighted Dialog.

Faunus.   *Faunus,* His Jolly Savage.

Genius loci.   *Genius loci,* His tempring of all things within and without, with apt time and place to pleazure and delight.

Charites.   Then the three *Charites:* [or Graces:] *Aglaia,* with her lightfum gladnes. *Thalia,* her floorifhing frefhnes, *Euphrofyne,* her cheerfulnes of Spirite, and with thefe three *Concordia,* with her Amitee and good agree-men!. That too hoow great effeEts their poours wear pooured oout hear among us, iet it bee judged by this, that by a multytude thus met of a three or foour thoufand every day: and diverz dayz more, of fo fundry degreez, profeffionz, Agez, Appetytz, dif-

pozitions

pozitions and affectionz; fuch a drifte of
tyme waz thear paffed, with fuch amitee,
loove, paftime, agreement, and obediens
whear it fhoold; and without Quarrell, jarr-
ing, grudging, or (that I coold hear) of yll
woord between any. A thing *Mafter Martin*
very rare and ftraunge, and yet no more
ftraunge then tru.

The *Parcæ*, (as earft I fhoold have faid) The *Parcæ*
the firft night of her *Majeftiez* cumming, they
heering and feeing fo precioous ado heer at
a place unlookt for, in an uplondifh Cuntree
fo far within the Ream: preaffing intoo e-
very fteed whear her highnes went, whearby fo duddld with fuch varietee of delyghts,
did fet afide their Hufwifrye, and coold not
for their harts tend their Work a whyt. But
after they had feen her *Majefty* a bed, gat
them a prying into every place: Olld Hags!
az fond of Nuelltiez, az yoong girls that had
never feen Coourt afore: but neyther full
with gazing, nor weary with gadding; leaft
off yet for that time, and at high midnight
gate them gigling, (but not a looud) into
the prezens chamber: minding indeed with
their prezent diligens, too recompens their
former flaknes.

I   So,

So, fetting themfelvez thus dooun too their woork, Alas! Sayz *Atropos*, I have loft my Sheerz: *Lachefis* laught apace and woold not draw a threed: And think ye damez that ile hoold the diftaff, whyle both ye fit idle? why no, by my Moother's foll quoth *Clotho*. Thearwith fayr lapt in a fine lawn the Spindel and rok, that waz dizend with pure purpl fylk, layd they fafely up toogyther: That other *Majefliez* diftaff, for an eighteen dayz, thear waz not a thread Spoon I affure you. The too Syfters after that (I hard fay) began their woork again that long may they continu: but *Atropos* hard no tyding of her Sheers, and not a man that moned her lofs. Shee iz not beloved furely; for this can I tell yoo, that whither it bee for hate too the Hag, or loove to her Highnefs, or els for both; every man prayz *God* fhe may never find them for that woork, and fo pray I daily and duly with the devouteste.

Thus partly ye perceyve now, hoow greatly the *Gods* can do for mortals, and hoow mooch alwey they loove whear they like: that what a gentl *Jove* waz thys, thus curteoofly too contrive heer fuch a treyn of
Gods?

Gods? Nay then rather *Mafter Martin* (to cum oout of oour Poeticaliteez, and too talk no more ferioous tearms,) what a magnificent *Lord* may we juftly account him, that cold fo highli caft order for fuch a *Jupiter* and all hiz Gods befid: That none with hiz influens, good property or prezent wear wanting; but alweiz redy at hand, in fuch order and aboundans for the honoring and delight of fo high a Prins, oour moft gracious *Queen* and Soverain. A Prins (I fay) fo finguler in preeminence, and worthines aboove al other Princez and digniteez of oour time: thoogh I make no comparifon too yearz paft, to him that in this point, either of ignorauns,——(if any fuch can be,) or els of malevolens woold make any doout: fit liber Indez (as they fay) let him look on the matter, and aunfwer himfelf, he haz not far to travell.

Az for the amplitude of his *Lordfhips* mynde, albeit that I poor foll can in conceit no more attain untoo, then judge of a Gem whearof I have no fkill: ye, thoogh dayly worn and refplendant in myne Ey: Yet fum of the Vertuze and propertiez thearof, in quantitee or qualitee fo apparaunt az can-

nqt

not be hidden but feen of all men, moought
I be the boolder to reaport hereunto yoo: but
as for the valu, yoor jewellers by their carrets
let them caft and they can.

And fyrft, who that confiderz untoo the
Stately feat of *Kenelwoorth Caftl,* the rare
beauty of Bilding that hiz Honor hath a-
vaunced; all of the hard quarry ftone: every
room fo fpacioous, fo well belighted, and fo
hye roofed within: fo feemly too fight by
due proportion without: a day tyme on
every fide fo glittering by glaffes; a nights,
by continuall brightneffe of Candel, fyre,
and torch-light tranfparent thro the lyght-
fom wyndoz, az it wear the *Egiptian Pharos*
relucent untoo all the *Alexandrian* Coaft:
or els, (too talke merily with my mery freend,)
thus radiaunt, az thoogh *Phœbus* for hiz eaz
woold reft him in the *Caftl,* and not every
night fo to travel doown untoo the *Antipodes.*
Heertoo fo fully furnifht of rich Apparell and
Utenfilez apted in all pointes to the beft.

*Kenelworth
Caftle
defcriv'd.*

Untoo thiz, hiz honorz exquifit appointment of a beautiful Garden, an Aker or
more of quantitee, that lyeth on the North
thear: Whearin hard all along the *Caftl*
wall

The Garden.

wall iz reared a pleazaunt Terras of a ten
foot hye, and twelve brode; eeven under
foot, and frefh of fyne Grafs; az is alfo the
fyde thearof toward the Gardien, in whiche,
by fundry equall diftauncez: With Obelifks
and fphearz, and white Bearz, all of ftone
upon theyr curioous bafez, by goodly fhew
wear fet: too theez, too fine arbers redolent
by fweet trees and floourz, at ech end one,
the garden plot under that, with fayr alleyz
green by grafs, eeven voided from the bor-
derz a both fydez, and fum (for chaunge)
with fand, not light or too foft or foilly by
duft, but fmooth and fyrme, pleafaunt too
walk on, az a fea-fhore when the Water iz
availd: then, much gracified by du proporcion of four eeven quarterz: In the midft
of each, upon a bafe a two foot fquare, and
hye, feemly borderd of it felf, a fquare
pilafterrizing pyramidally of a fyfteen foot
hye: Simmetrically peerced through from
a foot beneath, untill a too foot of the top:
whearupon, for a Capitell, an Orb of a ten
inches thik: Every of theez, (with hiz
bafe,) from the groound too the top, of one
hole peece; heawen out of hard porphiry,
and with great art and heed (think me) thy-
ther conveyd and thear erected. Whearat,
further

further allſo, by great caſt and coſt, the
ſweetneſs of favoour on all ſidez, made ſo
reſpiraunt from the redolent plants and fragrant earbz and floourz, in foorm, cooler,
and quantitee ſo delicioufly variant; and
frute treez bedecked with their Applz, Peares
and ripe Cherryez. .

The Cage, or Aviary. And unto theez, in the midſt, agaynſt the
Terres, a ſquare Cage, ſumptuoous and
beautifull, joyned hard to the north wall
(that a that ſide gards the Garden, as the
Gardein the *Caſtl*) of a rare form and excellency was reyzed: in heyth a twentye
foot, thyrty long, and a foourteen brode.
From the ground ſtrong and cloſe, reared
breaſt hye, whearat a ſoyl of a fayr moold-
ing was coouched all aboout: from that
upward, foour great Wyndoz a froont, and
too at each eend, every one a five foot wyde
az many mo eeven above them, divided on
all parts by a tranſam and architrave, ſo
likewize raunging aboout the Cage. Each
Windo arched in the top, and parted from
oother ceven diſtauns by flat fayr bolteld
columns, all in foorm and beauty like, that
ſupported a cumly corniſh couched al along
upon the bole ſquare. Which with a wire
net,

net, finly knit, of mafhez fix fquare, an inch
wide (az it wear for a flat roof) and like-
wyfe the fpace of every Windo with great
cunning and cumlinefs, eeven and tight waz
ail over-ftrained. Under the Cornifh again,
every part beautifyed with great Diamons,
Emerauds, Rubyes, and Saphyres: poynted,
tabld, rok and roo, and garnifht with their
golld, by fkilful hed and hand, and by toile
and penfil fo lyvely expreft, az it mought
bee great marveil and pleazure to confider
how neer excellency of Art could approch
untoo perfeftion of Nature.

Bear with me good cuntreeman, thoogh
thingez be not fheeawd heer az well az I
woold, or az well az they fhoold. for indeed I can better imagin and conceyve that
I fee, then well utter or duly declare it.
Holez wear thear alfo and caverns in orderly diftauns and facion, voyded intoo the wall
az well for heat, for coolnes, for rooft a
nightz and refuge in weather, az allfo for
breeding when tyme iz. More, fayr eeven
and frefh hollye treez for pearching & proin-
ing, fet within, tooward each eend one.

Heerto, their diverfitee of meats, their
fine

fine feveral veffels for their water and fundry
grainz; and a man fkilful & diligent to looke
to them and tend them.

But fhall I tell yoo the filver foounded
Lute, withoout the fweet toouch of hand:
the glorioous goollden cup, withoout the frefh
fragrant wine, or the rich ring with gem,
without the fayr feawtered finger; is nothing
indeed in his proper grace and ufe: even
fo his Honor accounted of this Manfion,
'till he had plaft thear tenauntes according.
Had it thearfore replenifhte with lively
Burdz, *Englifh, French, Spanifh, Canarian,*
and (I am deceaved if I faw not fum) *Afri-*
can. Whearby, whither it becam more de-
lightfum in chaunge of tunez, and armony
too the Eare; or els in differens of coolerz,
kindez, and propertyez too the Ey, Ile tell
yoo If I can, when I have better bethought
me.

The Gardiner. One day *(Mafter Martin)* az the Gardin
door waz open, and her highnes a hunting,
by licens of my good freend *Adrian,* I cam
in at a bek, but woold fkant oout with a
thruft: for fure I waz loth fo foon to depart.
Well may this *(Mafter Martyn)* bee fumwhat
too

too magnitude of mynde, but more thearof az ye fhall kno, more cauz ye fhall have fo to think: heer out what I tell yoo, and tell me when we meet.

In the Center (az it wear) of this goodly Gardein, waz theer placed a very fayr Foountain, caft intoo an eight fquare, rear- *The Fountain.* ed a four foot hye; from the midft whearof a colum up fet in fhape of too Athlants joined togeather a back half; the toon looking Eaft, toother Weft, with theyr hands uphollding a fayr formed Boll of a three foot over; from wheance fundrye fine Pipez did lively diftill continuall ftreamz intoo the receyt of the foountayn,———maiteyned ftill too foot deep by the fame frefh falling Water: whearin pleazaunly playing too and fro, and round about, Carp, Tench, Bream, and for Varietee, Pearch and Eel, fifh fayr liking all, and large: In the top, the ragged Staff; which, with the Boll, the Pillar, and eyght fidez beneath, wear all heawen oout of rich and hard white marbl. A one fyde, *Neptune* wyth hiz Tridental Fufkin triumphing in his Throne, trayled into the Deep by his marine horfez. On another, *Thetis* in her Chariot drawn by her Dolphins. Then

K   *Triton*

Triton by hiz Fiſhez. Heer *Protheus* herding hiz Sea buls. Thear *Doris* and her doughterz folacing a fea & fandz. The Wavez foourg-ing with froth and fome, entermengled in place, with Whalez, Whirlpoolz, Sturgeonz, Tunneyz, Conchs, and Wealks, all engraven by exquifit devize and ſkill, ſo az I maye

thinke this not much inferioour untoo *Phœbus* gatez, which (*Ovid* fayz) and peradventur a pattern to this, that *Vulcan* himſelf dyd cut: whearof fuch waz the excellency of Art, that the woork in valu furmoounted the ſtuff, and yet wer the gatez all of clean maſſy fylver.

Heer wear thinges ye fee moooght inflame ony mynde too long after looking: but whoo fo was found fo hot in defyre, with the wreaſt of a cok waz fure of a coolar: water fpurting upward with fuch vehemency, az they ſhoold by and by be moyſtned from top too toe; the Hee's to fum laughing, but the ſhee's to more fport: This fumtime waz Occupied to very good paſtime.

A Garden then fo appoynted, az whear-in aloft upon fweet ſhadoed walk of terras, in heat of foomer, too feel the pleazaunt

whiſking

whifking wynde above, or deleɛtabl coolnes
of the foountain fpring beneath: to tafte of
delicious Strawberiez, Cherryez, and oother
frutez, eeven from their ftalks: too fmell
fuch fragrancy of fweet Odoourz, breathing
from the plants, earbs and floourz: too heer
fuch natural melodioous muzik and tunez of
burdz: to have in Ey, for myrth fumtime
theez underfpringing ftreamz: then, the
Woods, the Waters, (for both pool and
chafe wer hard at hand in fight,) the Deer,
the Peepl (that oout of the Eaft arber in the
bafe Coourt, alfo at hande in view) the frute
trees, the plants, the earbs, the floowers,
the chaunge in coolerz, the Burds flyttering,
the fountain ftreaming, the Fyfh fwymming,
all in fuch deleɛtabl varietee order dignitee;
whearby, at one moment, in one place, at
hande, without travell, to have fo full fruition
of fo many *God's* bleffinges, by entyer delight unto all fenfez (if al can take) at once:
for *Etymon* of the woord woorthey to bee   *Paradifus*
Græc.
calld *Paradys:* and though not fo goodly as   *Hortus*
amænifh. aut
as *Paradis* for want of the fayr Rivers, yet *Hebraе. Pardes*
better a great deel by the lak of fo unhappy *ideft Hortus.*
a tree.   Argument moft certein of a right
noble mynde, that in this forte coold have
thus all contrived.

K 2

But

But *Mafter Martin*, yet one wyndlefs muft I featch, too make ye one more fayr coorz The Number One. and I can: and cauz I fpeak of One, let me tell yoo a littl of the dignitee of One-hood; whearin allweys al by Deitee al Soveraintee, preeminens, principalitee and concord with-oout poffibilitee of difagreement is conteyn-ed: As One God, One Savioour, One Feith, One Prins, One Sun, One Phœnix; and az One of great Wizdom Sayz, One hart, One Wey. Whear One-hood reinz, ther quiet bears rule, and difcord fliez a pafe. Three again may fignify cumpany; a meet-ing, a multitude, pluralitee; fo az all talez and numbrings from two unto three, and fo upward, may well be counted numberz, 'till they moount untoo infinitee, or els too confufion, which thing the fum of two can never admit; nor it felf can well be coount-ed a number, but rather a freendly con-junaction of two Ones; that keeping in a fynceritee of accord, may purport untoo us Charitee each too Other; mutual Love, agree-ment and integritee of freendfhip without Diffimulation. Az in theez: The two Tefta-ments; the Two tables of the Law; The Two great Lights, Duo luminaria magna, the Sun and Moon. And, but mark a littl

I pray

I pray, and fee how of all things in the
World, oour toongs in talk doo alweys fo
redily trip upon Two's, Payrs, and Couples:
Sumtymez az of things in Equality, fumtime,
of Differens, Sumtime of Contrariez, or for
Comparyzon, but cheefly for the moft part,
of things that between themfelvez do well
agree, and are faft linked in Amitee: Az
fyrft for Paftimez Hooundz and Hawks;
Deer red and fallo; Hare and Fox; Part-
rich and Fezaunt; Fifh and Fooul; Carp
and Tench. For Wars, Speer and Sheeld;
Hors and Harnefs; Swoord and Buckler.
For Suftenauns, Wheat and Barley; Peas
and Beanz; Meat and Drink; Bread and
Meat; Beer and Ale; Applz and Pearz.

But leaft by fuch Dualiteez I draw you
too far; let us here ftay and cum neerer
home. See what a fort of freendlie *Binitee'z*
we oour felvez do confift and ftond upon:
Fyrft our Two feet, Two Legs, Two kneez,
fo upward: and Above, Two Shoolderz,
Two Arms, and Two Hands. But cheefly
oour principl Two; that iz, Body and Soll:
Then in the Hed, whear all our Senfez meet,
and almoft all in Two's: Two Nozethrills,
Two Earz, and Two Eyz: So ar we of
freendly

freendly Two's from top to toe. Wel, to this Number of *Binitee'z*, take ye One mo for an Upſhot, and heer an eend.

The 2 Dials. Two Dials nye unto the Battilments are ſet aloft upon two of the Sydes of *Cæſar's* Tower; one Eaſt, the oother South; for ſo ſtond they beſt to ſheaw the Hoourz to the Tooun and Cuntree: both fayre large and *blew Biſe.* rich, by byſe for ground, and Goold for letters, whearby they glitter conſpicuous a great wey off. The Clok-bell that iz good and ſhrill, waz commaunded to Silens at firſt, and indeed ſang not a note all the while her Highneſs waz thear, the Clok ſtood allſo ſtill withall. But mark now, whither wear it by chauns, by conſtellation of Stars, or by fatal appoyntment (if fatez and Starz do deal with Dialz) thus waz it indeed: The handz of both the tablz ſtood firm and faſt, *The Dials* allweys pointing at two a Clok. Which *at 2 a Clok.* thing beholding by hap at fyrſt; but after ſeriouſly marking in deed, enprinted into me a deep ſign and argument certein: That this Thing amoong the reſt, waz for full Signifiauns of his *Lordſhips* honorabl, frank, freendly, and nobl hart towards all Eſtates: which whither cum they to ſtay and take cheer,

cheer, or ftraight to return: to fee, or to be feen: Cum they for Duty to her *Majefty*, or loove too his *Lordſhip*, or for both: Cum they early or late: for hiz *Lordſhips* part, they cum allweyz all at two a Clok, een jump at two a Clok: that iz to fay, in good harte, good acceptauns, in amitee and freendlye wellcoom: who faw els that I faw, muft fay az I fay. For fo many things byfide----*Mafter Humphrey*, wear heerin fo confonant untò my conftruction, that this pointing of the Clok (to my felf) I took in amitee, as an Oracle certain. And heer is my wyndlefs, like yoor coorfe az pleaz ye.

But noow Syr too cum too eend. For receyving of her Highnefs, and entertainment of all thoother eftatez. Syns of Delicatez that oney wey moought fewe or delight; az of Wyne, Spice deynty Viaunds, place Muzik, Ornaments of hoous, rich Arras and Sylk (too fay nothing of the meaner thinges) the mafs by provizion waz heaped fo hoouge, which the boounty in fpending did after bewray. The conceit fo deep in cafting the plat at firft. fuch a wizdom and cunning in acquiring things fo rich, fo rare, and in fuch abundauns: by fo

imminent

imminent and profufe a charge of Expens,
whiche by fo honorabl fervis, and exquifit
Order, curteizy of Officerz, and humanitee
of all, wear fo bountifully beftoed and fpent;
what may this exprefs, what may this fet
oout untoo us, but only a magnifyk minde,
a finguler wizdoom, a prinfly purs, and an
heroical hart? If it wear my theam *Mafter
Martyn*, too fpeak of hiz *Lordfhips* greàt
honor and magnificens, though it be not in
mee too fay fufficientlie, az bad a pen-clark
az I am, yet coold I fay a great deel more.

But being heer now in magnificens, and
matterz of greatnes, It falls well too mynd
the great Tent. the greatnes of his Honor's Tent, that for
her *Majeflyez* dining waz pighte at long
Ichington, the day her Highnes cam to
Killingworth Caftl. A Tabernacl indeed for
number and fhift of large and goodlye roomz,
for fayr and eazy Officez both inward and
ooutward, al fo likefum in order and Ey-
fight: that juftly for dignitee may be com-
parabl with a beautifull Pallais; and for
greatnes & quantitee, with a proper Tooun,
or rather a Cittadell. But to be fhort, leafte
I keep you too long from the Ryall Ex-
chaunge noow, and too cauz yoo conceyve
mooche

mooche matter in feaweſt woordes. The
Iron bedſted of *Og* the king of *Baſan* (ye
wot) waz foour yards and a halfe long, and
two yards wide, whearby ye conſider a
Gyaunt of a great proportion waz he: This
Tent had feaven Cart lode of Pynz pertein-
ing too it: Noow for the greatneſs geſs az
ye can.

And great az it waz (to marſhall oour
matters of greatnes togither,) not forgetting a
Weather at *Grafton,* brought too the Coourt,
that for body and wool waz exceeding great;
the meazure I tooke not: let me ſheaw you
with what great marvel a great Chyld of
Leyceterſhire, at this long *Ichington,* by the
Parents waz prezented: great (I ſay) of limz
and proportion, of a foour foot and foour
inches hye; and els lanuginoous az a lad of
eyghteen yearz, being indeed——avowd too
be but ſix yeer old; nothing more bewray-
ing hiz age, then hiz wit; that waz, az for
thooz yeers ſimpl and childiſh.

Az for unto hiz *Lordſhip,* having with ſuch
greatnes of honorabl modeſty and benignitee
ſo paſſed foorth, az Laudem ſine Invidia &
amicos pararit. By greatneſse of well doo-
L   ing

Deut. 3.

Terent.

ing, woon with all forts to bee in fuch re-
Blas. verens az De quo mentiri fama veretur: In
fynceritee of freendſhip ſo great, az no man
Ovid. more devooutly woorſhips. Illud amicitiæ
fanctum & venerabile nomen. So great in
Liberalitie, az hath no wey to heap up the
maſs of hiz Trezure, but only by liberal gyv-
ing and boonteoous beftowing hiz trezure:
folding (az it feemez) that faw of Martial that
fayth,

Martial.   Extra fortunam eft, quicquid donatur amicis;
     Quas dederis, folas femper habebis opes.
Oout of all hazerd do'ſt thou fet that to thy freends thou giveſt:
A furer Trezure canſt thou not have ever whyle thoou lyveſt.

what may theez greatneſſes bode, but only az
great honor, fame & renooun for theez parts
heer awey, az ever waz untoo thoz two nobl
Greatz: the *Macedonian Alexander* in *Ema-
thia* or *Grees,* or to *Romane Charles* in *Ger-
manye* or *Italy?* which, wear it in me ony
way to fet oout, no man of all men by *God*
(*Maſter Martin*) had ever more cauz, and
that heerby confider yoo.

It pleazed hiz Honor to beare me good
wil at fyrſt, and ſo too continu. To have
given me apparail eeven from hiz bak, to
get me allowauns in the Stabl, to advauns
                                     me

me untoo this woorfhipful Office fo neer the
moft honorabl Councell, to help me in my
Licens of Beanz (though indeed I do not
fo much uze it, for I thank *God* I need not)
to permit my good *Father* to ferve the ftabl.
Whearby I go now in my fylks, that elfe
might ruffl in my cut Canves: I ryde now
a hors back, that els many timez mighte
mannage it a foot: am knoen to their honors,
and taken foorth with the beft; that els
might be bidden to ftand bak my felf: My
good *Father* a good releef, that hee farez
mooch the better by, and none of theez for
my dezert, eyther at fyrft or fins, *God* he
knoez. What fay ye my good freend *Humphrey*, fhoold I not for ever honor, extol
him all the weys I can? Yes, by your leave,
while *God* lends me poour to utter my minde.
And, having az good cauz of hiz Honor,
az *Virgil* had of *Auguftus Cæfar*, will I poet
it a littl with *Virgil*, and fay

> Namque erit Ille mihi femper Deus, illius aram
> Sæpe tener noftris ab Ovilibus imbuet agnus.

*Virgib.
Eclog.* 1.

For he fhall be a *God* to me, 'till death my life confumes,
Hiz Auterz will I Sacrifize with incens and parfumez.

A fingular patron of humanitee may he be
well unto us towarde all degreez: of Honour,
toward hye Eftates, and cheeflye whearby
we may learne in what dignitee, worfhip and

reverens

reverens her Highnes is to be efteemed, honored and received, that waz never indeed more condignly done than heer; fo az neyther by the Builders at firft, nor by the Edict of pacification after, waz ever *Kenelworth* more nobled, than by thys hiz *Lordfhip's* receiving hir Highnes heer now.

1266
An.50.Hen.3.

But *Jefu Jefu* whither am I drawen noow. But tallk I of my *Lord* onz, een thus it farez with me: I forget all my freends, and my felf too. And yet yoo, being a Mercer, a Merchant, az I am: My Cuntreeman born, and my good freend withall, whearby I kno ye are compaffiond with me: methought it my part fumwhat to iimpart unto yoo, hoow it iz heer with me, and hoow I lead my life, which indeed iz this. viz.

A Mornings I rize ordinarily at feaven a Clok: Then reddy, I go intoo the Chappell: foon after eyght, I get me commonly intoo my *Lord's* Chamber, or intoo my *Lords* prezidents. Thear at the Cupboord after I haven eaten the Manchet, ferved over night for livery, (for I dare be az bolld, I promis yoo, az any of my freends the Servaunts thear: and indeed coold I have frefh, if I
woold

woold tarry, but I am of woont jolly and
dry a mornings:) I drink me up a good bole
of Ale: when in a fweet Pot it iz defecated
by al night's ftanding, the drink iz the better,
take that of me: and a morfel in a Morn-
ing, with a found draught, is very holfome
and good for the Ey-fight: Then I am az
frefh all the forenoon after, az had I eaten
a hole pees of beaf. Noow Syr, If the
councell fit, I am at hand; wait at an inch
I warrant yoo: If any make babling, "peas
(fay I) woot ye whear ye are? If I take a
lyftenar, or a pryer in at the chinks or at
the lok-hole, I am by and by in the bones
of him: But now they keep good order,
they kno me well inough: If a be a freend
or fuch a one az I lyke; I make hym fit
dooun by me on a foorm or a cheaft: let the
reft walk a *God's* name.

And heer doth my langages now and than
ftond me in good fted: My *French*, my
Spanifh, my *Dutch*, and my *Latten:* Sumtime amoong Ambaffadours men, if their
Mafter be within with the Councel: Sumtime with the Ambaffador himfelf, if he bid
call his lacky, or afk me what's a Clok; and
I warrant ye I aunfwer him roundly; that
they

they marvel to fee fuch a fellow thear: then
laugh I and fay nothing. Dinner and Sup-
per I have twenty placez to go to, and hart-
ly prayd to: Sumtime get I to *Mafter Pin-
ner;* by my faith a worfhipfull Gentleman,
and az careful for hiz charge az ony her
highneſ hath: thear find I allways good
Store of very good Viaunds; we eat and bee
merry, thank *God* & the *Queen.* Himfelf in
feeding very temperat & moderat az ye fhall
fee ony: and yet, by your leave, of a difh,
as a Colld Pigeon or fo, that hath cum to
him at meat more than he lookt for, I have
feen him een fo by and by Surfit, az he hath
pluct off hiz Napkin, wyept his knife, and eat
not a morfel more: lyke ynoough to ftick
in hiz ftomake a two dayz after: (fum hard
meſſage from the higher Officers; perceive ye
me?) Upon fearch, hiz faithful dealing and
diligens hath found him fautles.

In afternoons and a nights, fum time am
I with the right woorfhipfull *Sir George
Howard,* az good a Gentlman az ony livez:
And fumtime, at my good *Lady Sid-
neis* Chamber, a Noblwooman that I am
az mooch bound untoo, az ony poore
man maye be untoo fo gracyoous a Lady:
and

and fumtime in fum oother place. But
alwayez among the Gentlwemen by my
good will; (O, yee kno that cum alweyez
of a gentle Spirite:) And when I fee cumpany according, then can I bee az lyvely too:
Sumtime I foote it with Dauncing: noow
with my Gittern, and els with my Cittern, *Guittarr.*
then at the Virgynalz: Ye kno nothing cums
amiffe to mee: Then Carroll I up a Song
withall: That by and by they cum flocking
about me lyke Beez too hunny: And ever
they cry, anoother, good *Langham*, anoother! Shall I tell yoo? when I fee *Miſterz*
——(A, fee a mad Knave; I had almoſt
tollde all!) that fhe gyvez onz but an Ey,
or an Ear: why then, Man, am I bleſt; my
grace, my corage, my cunning is doobled:
She fayz, Sumtime, She likez it; and then I
like it mooch the better; It dooth me good to
heer hoow well I can doo. And too fay truth;
what with myne Eyz, az I can amorooufly
gloit it, with my *Spaniſh* Sofpires, my *French*
Heighes, mine *Italian* dulcets, my *Dutch*
hovez, my doobl releas, my hye reaches, my
feyning, my deep Diapafon, my wanton
warblz, my running, my tyming, my tuning,
and my twynkling, I can gracify the matters
az well az the prowdeſt of them, and waz
yet

yet never ſtaynd I thank *God:* By my troth,
Cuntreman, it iz ſumtim by midnight, e'er
I can get from them. And thus have I told
ye moſt of my Trade, al the leeve long daye:
what will ye more, *God* ſave the *Queen,* and
my *Lord.* I am well I thank yoo.

Heerwith ment I fully to bid ye farewell;
had not this doubt cum to my minde, that
heer remains a doout in yoo, which I ought
(methought) in any wyze to cleer. Which,
iz, Ye marvel perchauns to ſee me ſo book-
iſh. Let me tell yoo, in few woords: I went
to Scool, forſooth, both at *Pollez,* and allſo
at *Saint Antoniez:* In the fifth foorm, paſt
Eſop fabls, I wys, (and) red *Terens,* vos iſtæc
intro auferte, and began with my *Virgill*
Tytire tu patulæ. I coold my rules conſter
and pars with the beſt of them ſyns: Then,
as partly ye kno, have I traded the feat of
Marchaundize in ſundry Cuntreys, and ſo
gat me Languages: which do ſo littl hinder
my *Latten,* az (I thank God) have mooch
encreaſt it. I have leizure ſumtime, when
I tend not upon the Councell; whearby, now
look I on one book, noow on an other.
Storiez I delight in: the more auncient and
rare, the more like-ſum unto me: If I tolld
ye,

ye, I lyked *William a Malmefbery* fo well,
bicauze of hiz diligenz and antiquitee, perchauns ye woold confter it bicauz I love
Mamzey fo well: But I feith it iz not fo:
for fipt I no more Sak and Suger, (and yet
never but with company,) then I do *Malmzey*,
I fhoold not blufh fo mooch a dayz az I doo:
ye kno my minde.

Well noow, thus fare ye hartily well
yfeith: If with wifhing it coold have bin,
ye had had a Buk or two this foomer; but
we fhall cum neerer fhortly, and then fhall
we merreley meet and grace o' God. In the
mean time, commend me I befeech yoo, untoo my good freends, almoft moft of them
yoor Neighbourz: *Mafter Allderman Pulli-
fon*, a fpecial freende of mine: And in ony
wife too my good old freend *Mafter Smith*,
Cuftumer, by that fame token,——"Set my
hors up to the rack, and then lets have a
Cup of fak. He knoes the token well ynough,
and will laugh, I hold ye a grote. Too
Mafter Thorogood: and to my mery cum-
panion (a Mercer ye wot az we be) *Mafter
Denman*, Mio fratello in Chrifto: He iz
woont too fummon me by the Name of
Ro. La. of the Coounty *Nofingham* Gentle-

M   man :

man: A good Companion I feyth. Well,
Onez again fare ye hartely well. From the
Coourt. At the Citee of *Worceter*, the XX of
Auguſt 1575.

Yor Countreeman, Companion, & freend
aſſuredly : Mercer, Merchant aventurer, and
Clark of the Councel Chamber door, and al-
ſo keeper of the fame :
El Prencipe Negro. par me R. L. Gent.
Mercer.

De Majeſtate Regia benigna.

Cedant Arma togæ, Concedat laurea linguæ,
  Jaðanter Cicero at juſtius illud habe :
Cedant Arma togæ, Vigil & toga cedat honori
  Omnia Concedant Imperioque ſuo.

Deo Opt. Max. Gratiæ.

F   I   N   I   S.